1000 REMARKABLE FACTS ABOUT BOOZE

1000 REMARKABLE FACTS ABOUT BOOZE

by Richard Erdoes

Original art by Richard Erdoes

rP

The Rutledge Press

New York, New York

Book design by Allan Mogel
Edited by Jay Hyams

Published by The Rutledge Press,
A Division of W. H. Smith Publishers Inc.,
112 Madison Avenue, New York, New York 10016

First Printing 1981
Printed in the United States of America

Library of Congress Cataloging in Publication Data

Erdoes, Richard.
1,000 remarkable facts about booze.

1. Alcoholic beverages—Popular works. I. Title.
TP507.E73 641.2'1'0973 81-7307
ISBN 0-8317-0958-8 AACR2

To all the jolly souls
who lift a glass to Bacchus
including my wife, Jean, who knows her wine
and can drink with the best

Contents

THE BITTER BREW: The history of beer

Babylonians sucking up beer

The first human being to get drunk was probably a Neolithic farmer somewhere between the Euphrates and Tigris rivers. Soaking germinating barley bread in water, he or she discovered beer making.

Both beer and wine date to the beginning of mankind, at least to a millennium or two before recorded history. There are slightly more indications that brews resembling beer preceded wine.

In 630 B.C. Diodorus of Sicily wrote that Osiris, an Egyptian pharaoh living around 2000 B.C., invented a fermented barley brew called *zythos*. However, beer had existed a long time before that.

In 2300 B.C. the Chinese quaffed a beerlike concoction called *kiu*.

Central American Indians made a sort of ale from corn. One of its chief ingredients was hairy caterpillars (skinned).

The oldest existing Sumerian clay tablet, from about 6000 B.C., depicts ritual beer making for a temple festival. This sort of brew was "near" beer, weak and sweetish. That hops give beer its pleasing bitter tang was not discovered until much later on. Sumerians had to drink a lot of beer to get drunk, but they managed.

By 4000 B.C. Sumerian drinkers could choose among 16 different varieties of beer.

Beer was one of the main products of ancient Mesopotamia. Forty percent of the grain harvest was devoted to its manufacture.

Workmen building a Sumerian temple received a daily ration of 2½ pints of beer. Overseers and priests received 6 times that amount.

The inhabitants of Nineveh in Assyria were derided as alcoholics by the Prophet Nahum: "While they are drunken as drunkards, they shall be devoured, as stubble full dry." (Nah. 1:10)

In Mesopotamia the goddess Nin-Kashi, "She who fills the gullet," was the patroness of beer makers, the supernatural ale producer.

A Sumerian proverb says, "No pregnancy without copulation, no drunkenness without beer."

In the 18th century B.C., the great Babylonian king and lawgiver, Hammurabi, fixed punishments for tavern keepers who watered their product, sold beer that was too weak, and overcharged their customers.

Ancient Mesopotamians thought that old, cracked, and imperfectly covered beer jars made the finest brew. Such jars gave the bacteria a chance to give the beer a zest and a kick. The results were iffy—a gratifying hangover, a bad case of the runs, or sudden demise.

The deities of all germinating things were usually female; therefore, the earliest brewing was done by women.

About 3000 B.C. it was discovered that hops give beer a pleasant flavor. From that moment on, beer was really beer—a he-man's drink.

By 3000 B.C. 6 different types of beer were known in Egypt, the land of the pharoahs.

In 1200 B.C. the pharoah Ramses had it recorded that he had offered up to the gods no less than 466,303 pitchers of beer. The deities were properly grateful, showering boons upon their favorite pharoah.

According to Egyptian tradition, beer and wine were invented for humans by the goddess Isis.

Egyptian beer gardens of the 13th dynasty (around 1700 B.C.) served numerous kinds of beer made of barley steeped in water and fermented by natural yeasts mixed with germinating bread crumbs.

The ancient Egyptians thought that beer was good for a growing child. Therefore it was given to schoolboys to drink.

Egyptian lads were not the only ones to sample beer. Prussian schoolboys in the time of Frederick the Great and his father, Frederick William, the "Soldier King," were reared on *Bier Suppe* ("beer soup").

The word *beer* comes from the Germanic *peor* or *bior* (*bjor* in Scandinavian). *Peor* was a brew made from mashed, germinated barley.

The Latin word for beer, *cerevisia,* is derived from Ceres, the goddess of grain—grain being the raw material from which beer was made. *Cerveza* is the modern Spanish word for beer, *cerveja* the Portuguese.

A pot from the late Iron Age was found containing the residue of beer made from wheat and honey. The ancient Hochdeutsche term for this kind of strongly alcoholic stuff was *alo.* In Britain Anglo-Saxons called it *calu*—thus we got the word ale.

The Vikings called ale *oel.*

Dion Cassius, a Roman author, related, "The Pannonians, who inhabit the banks of the Danube, have neither oil nor wine. They eat barley and millet, and from these two kinds of grain they make a drink."

The Latin historian Ammianus Marcellinus mentioned a beer made in Illyria (modern Yugoslavia) called *sabaia.* He called the brew *liquore paupertinus*—"poor, weak liquor."

The ancient Greeks and Romans called all alcoholic beverages "wine." Beer was "barley-wine."

The Roman historian Tacitus wrote that beer had a certain resemblance to very bad wine and that it tasted sour. He also wrote that Germanic tribesmen were inordinately lazy, doing nothing but fighting and swilling down enormous quantities of beer. They got so drunk, Tacitus said, that under the influence they sometimes gambled or wagered their wives away.

Beer and mead got to the Germans and Scandinavians by way of the Celts or Gauls. Tacitus and other Roman writers speak of "The Great Celtic Thirst," which was proverbial.

Valhalla was the name of the Germanic pre-Christian heaven, accessible only to doughty warriors who had fallen in battle. Valkyries welcomed the slain fighters to Valhalla with enormous horns of beer or, as some say, mead.

As the ancient saga described Valhalla, the dead warriors did not suffer their wounds just to drink water: the goat Heidrun stood on the roof of Valhalla, and from her teats beer flowed, filling a vessel every day, a vessel so large that the warriors could get quite drunk out of it. Heidrun was an exceedingly useful goat.

Ancient Nordic laws forbade a husband to beat his wife, and because most men fell into this evil when drunk, the law made special provision that inebriation was no excuse.

The chief Nordic god, Odin, lived exclusively on mead and beer. He gave his food to his two pet wolves, who were teetotalers.

As the war god Ares was the mightiest drinker among the Greek pantheon, so hammer-wielding Thor was the champion guzzler among the Nordic deities.

Thor was once invited by the sorcerer Utgardaloki to a drinking bout. Thor was chagrined not to be able to empty the wizard's great drinking horn. Actually, Thor had not done so badly at all. The end of the horn had been plunged into the limitless sea, and even Thor could not swallow the whole ocean. He had, however, lowered the water level and thus caused the first ocean tides.

At a feast given by Thrym, the giant, Thor downed 3 large barrels of mead or beer—his usual measure.

Gambrinus was the medieval Flemish patron saint of beer. The name is a corruption of either Jan Primus ("John I"), a Burgundian prince who lived in the mid-13th century, or Jean sans Peur ("John the Fearless"), a duke of Burgundy who reigned in the late 14th century. Both were extremely partial to *bière*, which they consumed in great quantities. They were therefore mistakenly credited with having invented it.

The mighty baron Jan Primus once imbibed 72 quarts of beer during the course of one evening.

Jean sans Peur and Jan Primus might not have been the original Gambrinuses (or Gambrinii). A certain Aventinus maintains that Gambrinus was the husband of the Egyptian goddess Isis and lived somewhere around 1730 B.C. He is credited with the invention of a certain brew called *hek*.

In Bavaria and lower Austria, where much beer is drunk, one often encounters so-called *Marterls*, tablets erected on the spot where a poor beer tippler came to grief—as for instance falling from his wagon and breaking his neck while intoxicated. The tablets frequently bear the legend *Heiliger Gambrinus, bitt fuer uns!* ("Holy Gambrinus, pray for us"). Usually they also bear a naive painting graphically depicting the fatal mishap.

Images of St. Gambrinus are most often encountered in the section of Austria known as Inn Viertel, an area in which Hitler's birthplace is located. The local inhabitants are commonly called *Most* or *Bier Schaedel* ("beer heads").

The oldest German beer dates from A.D. 353. It was unearthed near Alzey in the Rhineland. An unappetizing, hardened black-brown mass, it can be admired at the Alzey Museum.

A favorite motif for 16th-century German engravers was a priest or monk quaffing mightily accompanied by the written legend, *"Ich trink fuer Alle!"* ("I drink for all!").

In the 18th century, Frederick the Great, also known as "*der Alte Fritz*," pushed beer in order to prevent his subjects from drinking coffee. Coffee was imported and therefore led to a loss of hard currency. Frederick hired so-called coffee sniffers to smell out violators of the anti-coffee law who were trying to evade the exorbitant taxes that the king had put on the divine mocha. The sniffers were all Frenchmen, because they had more delicate noses than the native Prussians (according to Frederick). "My subjects must drink beer," read a royal edict. "The king has been brought up on beer soup and so were his ancestors and his officers."

During the Franco-Prussian War of 1870, the German army laid siege to the city of Strasbourg. The citizens sent a request to General Uhlrich, the German commander, asking that he officially order the Prussians not to direct their artillery on their numerous breweries making good Alsatian beer. The Prussians complied, probably more out of self-interest than charity, as they were about to occupy the city.

Beer halls played an important role in Nazi Germany. The Nazi party was born inside the Sternecker Brauhaus. Early Nazi headquarters were the Munich Hofbrauhaus, the Buergerbrauhaus, the Thorbrau, the Arzberger Keller, and the Gonisl, a place famous for *Weisswurscht*, a sort of white and pale frankfurter. Under Hitler's rule the Buergerbrauhaus became a sort of Nazi shrine. It was there that, on November 8, 1923, Hitler launched his ill-fated beer-hall *Putsch*, a revolution by which he hoped to seize power in Germany and that brought him first to international attention.

Hitler started his *Putsch* by buying a *Maasskrug* of beer for 3 billion marks (Germany was at that time suffering terrible inflation). He then forced the heads of the Bavarian government at pistol point to join him. Hitler fired up the assembled crowd to a fever pitch by shouting, "*Bier her! Eins, zwei, drei, gsuffa!*" (Roughly translated: "Bring on the beer! One, two, three, down the hatch!")

Every year while the Nazi regime lasted, Adolf Hitler joined his old buddies at the Buergerbrauhaus on the 8th of November and made a

speech. In 1939 an anti-Nazi clockmaker, Georg Elser, planted a time bomb inside a pillar at a spot from which the Fuehrer used to harangue the crowd. It was set for 11:20 P.M. Hitler usually stayed until midnight. The bomb went off duly and on time, but Hitler had left an hour earlier than usual.

Bavarians are renowned beer drinkers. It is no wonder that the oldest still-functioning brewery is located at Freising in Bavaria. It was founded in 1040.

Koeniglichbayrischeroberbiersteuerhaupteinkassierer was the official title of a Bavarian collector of taxes on beer. Literally the word means "royal Bavarian superior beer-tax chief cashier." The title was abolished in 1918.

In one old Munich brauhaus the floor is made of marble and slants toward one corner, in which there is a hole. Burghers coming in for a long bout of heavy drinking arrived with their "piddling sticks." As the men's limbs grew heavy and their bladders full, rather than getting up, they urinated discreetly against their piddling sticks. The slanting floor did the rest. For similar purposes other Bavarians of old wore watertight leather breeches.

A certain Munich actor owned a Dackel ("dachshund") by the name of Buckshi. The animal insisted on his daily stein of beer. His favorite brand was Salvator Bier, dunkel. The dog was Bavarian, born and bred.

According to records dating from the turn of the century, one Bavarian drank 150 glasses of beer every day and, on a bet, one German-American of Cincinnati managed to swallow 188 glasses of beer between sunrise and sunset during one hot summer day (it is not known if he was of Bavarian ancestry).

Every autumn the world's most stupendous festival of beer guzzling takes place in the Bavarian city of Munich. The so-called *Oktoberfest* is held on Munich's Oktober Wiese, an immense fairground.

Munich, incidentally, means "monk." As elsewhere in medieval Europe, commercial beer brewing in Germany was first done in monasteries. Famous beers and beer halls bear the names of monastic orders: Franziskaner Brau or Augustiner Brau.

The most famous of all Munich beers is Muenchner Kindl, whose trademark is a little angel in a monk's habit.

Monks also distilled harder stuff—the Benedictines distilled the heavenly liquor named after them, the Carthusian monks created the far-famed Chartreuse.

The oddest of all German beers is a Berlin specialty—*Weiss Bier*. It neither tastes nor looks like beer. It is a colorless, highly carbonated liquid served in oversize glasses, and it tastes like sweet soda pop.

Bavarian waitresses toting good Bavarian brew

BRING US IN GOODE ALE: Beer in Britain

The very first wassail

Beer and ale came early to Merry Old England. The Greek writer Posidonius stated that the Celts brewed beer from grain and honey.

Pythias, a Massilian pilot who sailed to the British Isles in the 4th century, reported that the inhabitants made beer from grain and honey.

Beer made from heather was found in a prehistoric brewery in County Cork, Ireland.

According to Diodorus Siculus, the Sicilian historian, on festive occasions the ancient Britons drank intoxicating beverages made from honey, apples, and barley.

The Roman emperor Julian the Apostate called this early British beer "an offspring of corn, wine without wine."

The 1st-century Greek physician Dioscorides observed that the Britons and the Irish, instead of wine, used a beverage called *curmi*, made from barley. The English historian William Camden points out that *curmi* is a distortion of *cwrw*, the ancient Celtic word for ale.

The ancient Anglo-Saxon greeting *wa hael*, that is, "be well," became the yuletide *wassail*. Some say the word *ale* grew out of this.

According to Geoffrey of Monmouth, the annual custom of handing round the wassail bowl, as well as health-drinking, goes back to Hengist, leader of the Anglo-Saxon invasion of England. Hengist invited the British king Vortigern to a feast and ordered his daughter Rowena to welcome the guest at the door of the hall with a foaming bowl. She greeted Vortigern with a hearty "*Louerd king, wass-heil*," that is, "Be of good health, lord king." The British monarch, through an interpreter, replied, "*Drinc heile!*" ("Drink Health!"). This, according to Robert of Gloucester, was in "Englande the first was-hail."

Of the Irish St. Finnian, who died in A.D. 552, it was said: "Finnian was distinguished for his great sanctity and austere mode of living.

His usual food was bread and herbs; his drink water, but on festival days he used to indulge himself with a mug of beer."

St. Columba (A.D. 589–610) was also fond of beer and ale.

Both Saxons and Danes were mighty quaffers. There was an unwritten law that when a Saxon and a Dane were drinking out of the same bowl it would be a great dishonor for either to cut the other down with his scramasax or to poleax him. Murder had to wait until both were done drinking and well out of hall or inn.

William of Malmesbury wrote in the 12th century that the Saxons were accustomed to eating until bloated and drinking until they were sick.

William of Malmesbury also wrote of the Saxons that "They think they have not treated their guests well if they are not so full of drink that they vomit."

The Normans had a reputation for being abstemious, but only when compared with the Saxons. In the reign of Henry I, the Norman bishop of Ely every day served his guests—besides venison, fowl, and fish—wines from Aquitaine, spiced mead, sweet mulberry hippocras, pigmait (an unknown alcoholic beverage), cider, perry, and strong ale.

As Gilbert K. Chesterton put it:

St. George he was for England,
And before he killed the dragon
He drank a pint of English ale
Out of an English flagon

Ale was the most common English drink, "as needful to man as bread," as one writer put it. Laborers received a daily ration of ale as part of their wages. Some sort of beer was brewed in almost every English household.

By A.D. 800 beer and ale were brewed commercially in all monasteries, which became the chief suppliers. Each cloister produced its own distinctive brew. Most actually offered two types—great beer, strong and full-bodied, reserved for the good brothers and their favored guests at 1 gallon per day apiece; and small beer, for the common folk, poor pilgrims and such.

Although the malted drinks of Asia and the Mediterranean were based on barley, early English beer was manufacturered from oats.

Monks did not only brew the beer of Merry Old England, they also drank it copiously:

To drink like a Capuchin is to drink poorly,
To drink like a Benedictine is to drink deeply,
To drink like a Dominican is pot after pot,
But to drink like a Franciscan is to drink the cellar dry.

During the Great Fire of London, in September 1666, the conflagration reached the Temple, once the abode of the Knights Templars, but at that time a court of law. The lawyers extinguished the flames with ale from their ample cellars.

Ale was the festive drink of England, a symbol of merrymaking. There were Bridals (Bride-ales) for the wedding feast; Church-ales, to raise money for the clergy; Leet-ales, celebrated on leet, or manorial, day; Whitsun-ales; Lamb-ales, at shearing time; Bid-ales (Benefit-ales); and many more.

Grave-ales were held to console widows and orphans. Some wakes were not altogether doleful.

English universities had their special festivals, called College-ales. Some colleges brewed their own ales. Some of these famous and venerable concoctions still tickle Britannic throats, such as Audit ale from Cambridge, Archdeacon from Merton College, and Chancellor from Queen's College, Oxford.

Among crimes punished with the ducking stool in the city of Chester during Saxon times was the brewing of bad and weak beer.

In those brave days of old, men sang at their tables:

Bring us in no beef, for there is many bones;
Bring us in Goode Ale, for that goes down at once.
Bring us in no eggs, for there be many shelles;
But bring us in Goode Ale, and give us nothing else!

To prevent poor-quality brews, the job of ale conner was created—according to some historians as early as Norman times. Ale conners were expert tasters who sampled specimens, pronouncing on their wholesomeness or strength. If a batch of ale was too weak, it was condemned and had to be sold at half price. Ale conners were often paid in kind, that is, in beer. William Shakespeare's father is supposed to have been an ale conner, among other things.

Unfortunately, taxes—especially taxes in some way connected with alcoholic beverages—are almost as old as drinking itself. In the year 694 Ina, king of Wessex, decreed that everyone who possessed a farm of 10 hides of land should pay him 12 ambers of Welsh beer. An amber contained 7 English gallons. *Ealu* was what Ina called his ale.

In early England one could pay one's taxes in kind. For tax purposes 1 cask of mead was worth 2 casks of spiced ale or 4 casks of common ale.

It was King James I who hit upon the scheme of selling licenses to beer vendors, thereby fattening his exchequer and increasing the price of England's favorite refreshment. James I was not a popular king.

The English Crown fixed the price of beer and ale as early as 1226. Government, it was said, had a big nose that it liked to stick into the liquor business.

Oliver Cromwell passed an ordinance by which persons who had overindulged "in any Inne, Ale house or Victualling house" were to be punished by a fine of 5 shillings.

Some drinkers were "undone" by "strong beere" due to the gargantuan quantities quaffed. One medieval Lord Mayor of London consumed 1 gallon of strong ale as an eye-opener with every breakfast for 24 years.

Good Queen Bess downed 2 large bumpers of beer every morning.

Mary Stuart was a hearty drinker. Secret messages were smuggled to her in waterproof pouches inside casks of beer while she was held captive by Elizabeth.

At an entertainment given by the Earl of Leicester at Kenilworth Castle for Queen Elizabeth, 365 hogsheads of beer alone were consumed. Assuming that 6,000 guests were present on the occasion, the stupendous quantity of 4 gallons would fall to the share of each person.

At the enthronment of one archbishop of York, more than 600,000 pints of beer were consumed.

The 16th-century writer Raphael Holinshed, commenting on the quaffing of "headie ale and beer," says, "They will drink till they be as red as cocks, and little wiser than their combs."

Working as a printer in London, Benjamin Franklin noted that his fellow workmen drank pints of ale all day. It was necessary, he supposed, to drink strong beer that they might be strong to labor.

The printing house where Franklin worked was located conveniently close to the Lincoln Inn. Franklin, who was abstemious when it came to ale (but not when it came to wine), was called by his English colleagues the "Water-American."

A certain Bill Lewis of Llandismaw, Wales, drank 8 gallons of ale every day before going to bed. One day he made the mistake of mixing his ale with equal parts of wine. This brought on a sudden colic that did him in. A special sort of crane had to be devised to lower him into his grave, as a lifetime of imbibing "headie ale" had increased his weight to over 500 pounds. Lewis, so eager mathematicians figured out, had consumed enough ale over the years to float a "Fourth Rate," that is, a 74-gun man-of-war.

Not to be outdone by the guzzlers in the brave old days, one John H. Cochrane, in 1932, downed 2 liters of beer (4.22 pints) in just under 11 seconds "in honor of Princeton University."

It was the addition of hops that brought about a clear differentiation between ale and beer, although hops were not used by English brewers before 1300.

Some modern British writers assert that hops were introduced to England by Flemish settlers in the 16th century.

Written records first mention hops as being used in the French monastery of St.-Germain-des-Près shortly after A.D. 800.

One author of old averred that "hops, reformation, bays and beer, came into England all in one year." Possibly he was a hermit living on an isolated island.

Whenever it began, "hoppy biere" quickly became a favorite, though some did not take to it at first. One 16th-century citizen complained that hopped beer was apt to kill a man suffering from the "colyck" and that one sample he tested was so clouded that it looked as if pigs had wrestled in it.

Whip-Belly- or Whistle-Belly-Vengeance was a fearful brew of 17th- and 18th-century Britain, Ireland, and English North America. It was sour household beer, sweetened with molasses, sprinkled with crumbs of "ryne-injun" bread, and boiled in a kettle. It was drunk scalding hot and had side effects hinted at by the name. Whistle-Belly-Vengeance was very popular in Salem, Massachusetts.

Most English beers are top brewed. The yeast stays on top of the brew during fermentation. Most European beers are bottom-brewed, that is, the yeast sinks to the bottom. Bottom-brewed beers are served chilled, or at least cold; top-brewed beer does not take kindly to chilling.

Irish stouts are served lukewarm even in summer, very tasty but hard on the kidneys. Stouts are dark, roasted-malt beers, somewhat sweet—except Guinness, which is somewhat between sweet and bitter.

A 17th-century traveler in England was impressed by the fact that there were more than 300 varieties of beer to be had.

White Shield, a Worthington beer, is bottled "live," that is, while still fermenting.

Whitbread's is particularly famous because it was first made by the founder in 1750. In 1787 George III (the one who "lost America") visited Whitbread's brewery.

The Dorchester Brewery, makers of Thomas Hardy's Ale, claims to make the strongest English beer, with more than 12 percent alcohol.

AT THE SIGN OF THE MERMAID: Inns, alehouses, and pubs in Merry Old England

Britons are as fond of their drinking houses as they are of the beer and ale they quaff in them. England is full of charming and venerable pubs, formerly known as inns, alehouses, and kiddleys, where beer has been guzzled for centuries.

Dr. Johnson said of British inns and alehouses: "No, Sir, there is nothing which has yet been contrived by man, by which so much happiness is produced as by a good tavern or inn."

There are many among the innumerable inns and pubs that claim to be the oldest. The title deeds of the Saracen's Head of Southwell go back to the year 1356. The place is supposed to have been given its name by crusaders who fought Saladin.

The Saracen's Head, Southwell

A Nottingham ballad rhapsodizes about one Dame Rose, who kept the Ram Ale House in that town "in the days of good King Stephen" (who reigned from 1135 to 1154).

The Fountain, in Canterbury, claims to be the place where the murderers of St. Thomas à Becket hatched their foul plot. It also claims that Edith Swan Neck, mistress of poor Harold, the last of the Saxon kings, stayed there in 1064.

Parts of the Bardsey, in Yorkshire, are said to go back to A.D. 953—parts only. Most of the structure is newer by centuries.

At the turn of this century the Fighting Cocks at St. Albans advertised itself as the oldest inhabited house in England. It once displayed a sign:

When Julius Caesar bided here,
He sampled our wine and beer.

Another signboard proclaimed: "Rebuilt After the Flood."

The Prospect of Whitby may be the oldest Thames-side pub in London. It hails from the time of Henry VIII.

There is no dispute as to which is the smallest pub in England. The prize for that goes to the Nutshell in Bury St. Edmunds, a very crammed place on a busy night. The Nutshell was once part of a pawnshop. Gentlemen could hock their watches or silk neckerchiefs and use the money to get soused. The decorative *pièce de résistance* is a 300-year-old stuffed cat.

The narrowest pub in the world is not in England, but in Amsterdam. It is called De Groene Lanteerne ("The Green Lantern"), and the entire building is less than 6 feet wide. Luckily it is considerably deeper. Among the heavenly liqueurs served at the Green Lantern are *Hemdje licht op* ("Lift your Nightshirt") and *Bruidstranen* ("Bride's Tears").

In most ancient British beerhouses, wine and ale were served from a special room or niche close to the porch called the *bower*, from the Danish *bür*, meaning "buttery." Thus we got the modern *bar.*

The word *pub* is derived from *public house,* another old name for an inn.

The man who serves the drinks in a pub is a *publican.*

Historic, bold, quaint, or humorous are the old names and signs by which the taverns and alehouses were known. Some of the names honor kings or the memories of battles. Such is the Crispin Crispinian Inn, which welcomed the troops of Henry V as they tramped along old Watling Road, after Agincourt, which was fought on the feast day of those twin saints.

The squalor of a taproom-cum-pawnshop

A surviving and very elaborate sign for the Six Alls tavern portrays a queen proclaiming, "I rule all," followed by a bishop with the legend, "I pray for all," then a lawyer, "I plead for all," followed by a doughty soldier announcing, "I fight for all," who in turn is followed by a taxpayer lamenting, "I pay for all." Last comes the devil, labeled, "I take all!"

There was no dearth of alehouses named "Cressy" (for Crécy), Agincourt, Poitiers, The Bull and Mouth (Boulogne Mouth, captured by Henry VIII), Gibraltar, Waterloo, Trafalgar, and Balaclava.

Some pubs were named after admirals, such as Drake, Blake, Albemarle, Nelson, and Beatty; some were named after generals and medieval captains, such as the Black Prince, the Great Harry, Marlborough, Iron Duke, Lord Raglan, Napier, Wolseley, Little Bobs (Field Marshal Roberts), Lord Kitchener, and Sir Douglas Haig.

Sharing a well-mixed bowl of punch

If an alehouse was named the Punch Bowl, it meant that the owner and clientele were Whigs. Whigs drank punch, possibly because it was favored by Charles James Fox. Tories drank port. Not a few taverns were named after statesmen and politicians.

Giving pubs names with political meaning was risky. After Richard III was defeated and killed at the Battle of Bosworth Field (1485), ending the Wars of the Roses, all the many White Rose inns changed their names because the white rose of York was Richard's symbol. Likewise, whenever the Lancastrians were losing, the Red Rose taverns were quickly renamed, though some owners said that the appellation "rose" meant the Virgin Mary.

With James I the name Unicorn came into use for taverns because this mythical beast's horn was supposed to detect poisons, and James considered himself threatened by plots to undo him with foul potions slipped into his drinks.

When Cromwell rose to power, the Rose and Crown, Knightsbridge, was promptly changed into the Oliver Cromwell. On the accession of Charles II, it just as quickly turned into the Rose and Crown again.

During the reign of Elizabeth I, many tavern keepers called their places Good Queen Bess or Queen's Head. Gloriana, the Virgin Queen, was easily offended if the portrait on a Good Queen Bess sign was not pretty enough for her. A queen's proclamation of 1563 complains that "a grete number of her loving subjects are muche greved and take grete offence with the errors and deformities allredy comitted by sondry persons in this behalf," and orders that measures be taken to "prohibit the shewing and publication of such signs as are apparently deformed, until they may be reformed which are reformable."

Many of the Queen's Head taverns are supposed to owe their existence to Sir Walter Raleigh, who obtained a patent "to make license for keeping of taverns and retailing of wines through England." Inside one of these Queen's Heads, at Islington, occurred an amusing incident in the early history of tobacco smoking. An attendant was horrified to observe a cloud of smoke issuing from Sir Walter's mouth. Thinking Raleigh to be on fire, he emptied a pail of strong beer over the head of the astonished knight.

London's Olde Cock tavern (sometimes a hangout for Samuel Pepys, who brought actresses and such there to "toy with") is famous for an unfortunate accident that befell one of the tavern's guests. The servant maids, thinking their master asleep, had made themselves a "posset, scalding and devilish hotte" in a large caldron, when suddenly they heard someone coming down the stairs. Fearing to be surprised by the innkeeper, they hastily lowered the devilish hot brew down the hole of the privy. "The sayd Gentleman, feeling the flux tormenting his Bowels, rose from his bedde to go to that place whence even the king walketh afoot, and, as it being darke, satte himself in the hot Posset and had his backside and cods sorely burnt, boilt and scalded, and the posset all spoylt, ruin't and defiled."

The Craven Head and the Cock and Magpie in London's Drury Lane saw royal Charles's mistress, Nell Gwyn, lifting one on occasion, no doubt flouting her fashionably exposed bosom (which had so inspired the king).

The Jolly Barber was an alehouse doubling as a barbershop. Jonathan Swift made a couplet on it that became the pub's motto:

Rove not from pole to pole, but step in here
Where nought excels the shaving but—the beer

The White Hart, in Drury Lane, was the place where the Great Plague of London made its first hideous appearance in the form of two Frenchmen with bloated and black faces who came in for a nip of brandy. The tapster, who recognized the Black Death when he saw it, immediately informed the innkeeper, but it was too late.

The London tavern Ye Olde Doctor Butler's Head was named for Dr. William Butler, the heavy-drinking physician of King James I. Butler invented a famous medicinal ale that cured most ailments, except epilepsy, which the doctor ministered to by suddenly, and without warning, firing off a brace of pistols close to the patient's ears.

Halting at the Castle Inn at Marlborough, a certain duke of Chandos heard loud maidenly screams. Investigating the matter, he found a beautiful girl being brutally beaten by the stablekeeper. The man explained to the duke that the girl was his wife and that therefore he could do with her what he pleased. He was, however, willing to sell her for 20 pounds. The duke paid the price and made the girl his duchess.

The tavern and alehouse keeper was called "Boniface," "ale-draper," and "Ganymede," but most often he was simply the "landlord."

The custom of calling a landlord "Boniface" is the result of a very popular play, *Beaux' Stratagem*, by George Farquhar, which featured a tavern keeper named Old Will Boniface.

One landlord named Daniel Lambert had a waistline of 9 feet and, supposedly, weighed 739 pounds. At his death, a wall of his pub had to be partially demolished to bring out his body. He is claimed to have been England's stoutest landlord.

Dirty Dick's is a London pub named after a former owner. After the death of his sweetheart, whom he was about to marry, he vowed never to wash himself again or clean up his public house. Dirty Dick was a man of his word.

In 1603 Sir Walter Raleigh formed the Mermaid Club. Among those who discussed literature inside the Mermaid Tavern were Shakespeare, Ben Jonson, and Keats.

HOPS ACROSS THE SEA: Beer in the New World

Sister Brady, famous for her extralarge pennyworths

The white man neither discovered America nor brought the first beer to the New World. People and beer were already there.

According to an 18th-century English author named Raynal, the Araucano Indians drank large quantities of a beer called Chicha, which they made from maize. "The elder females of the tribe prepare this beverage by chewing the maize, which they afterward collect in a trough resembling a canoe, and leave it to ferment. Previous to these feasts which end in premeditated intoxication, they voluntarily surrender their spears and knives to the women, who secrete them in the woods, as they are conscious of their propensity to quarreling and fighting when excited by drunkenness."

Some colonists did not wait for brewers out of Europe, but made their own ale from maize. Governor Oglethorpe declared it to be better than English beer.

The first European baby born in New Amsterdam was Johanna Vigne. She grew up to become a brewer.

The Dutch began brewing beer in 1612 in a crude stone building at the southernmost tip of Manhattan.

The first official commercial brewery in New Amsterdam was opened on what is now Wall Street. The lane leading up to the brewery was the first to be paved—it was paved so that heavy barrels could be more easily transported to and from it.

In 1623 the Virginia Assembly urged that all immigrants be constrained to bring with them a goodly supply of malt to be used in brewing, making it unnecessary to drink American water until their constitutions had become inured to the climate.

Jacobus, the first burgomaster of New Amsterdam, was a brewer. He opened his brewery in 1644. He also established the first beer garden in Old Knickerbocker Town.

In 1675 Cotton Mather lamented that every other house in Boston was an alehouse.

In 1609 Henry Hudson steered his good ship, the *Half Moon*, into New York Bay, landed on an island, and there treated some Indians to alcoholic beverages. The natives promptly named the island *Manahachtanienk*, which in time was simplified and spelled "Manhattan." It means "place where we all got drunk."

In 1548 English settlers made a premature attempt to found a colony in Virginia. The first thing they did was make beer from Indian corn.

In 1609 the governor and council of Virginia, in a pamphlet called *True and Sincere Declaration*, advertised for two brewers. The pamphlet was sent to England. In due time two Frenchmen arrived to fill the post. (English brewers did so well at home that none could be found willing to ply his trade in a far and barbaric land.) This was the first American "help wanted" ad.

The Pilgrims landed at Plymouth Rock, rather than at a more favorable place, because it was there that their beer gave out. As recorded in 1622, "For we could not now take time for further search or consideration; our victuals being much spent, especially our beer."

Two brothers, James and Jeffrey Dupper, were early brewers who, judging from all accounts, were the worst beer makers in the colonies. One George Sandys wrote in 1623 to a member of the council for the Virginia Company that "it would well please the Country to hear he had taken revenge of Dupper for his Stinking beer, which hath been the death of 200." There are several more contemporary letters that complain that the Dupper brothers' beer was killing great numbers of people.

By 1700, with the colonies barely some 80 years old and the number of white settlers well below 1 million, more than 10,000 people brewed, fermented, or distilled alcoholic beverages of a great

Upright Puritan displaying strict nattiness

variety. This accounted for only a small percentage of the alcohol consumed. Most of it was imported from the home country and the West Indies. The colonials had a mighty thirst—and not for water.

A popular drink in the colonies was a Yard of Flannel, an ale-based variety of hot flip.

Colonial New England taverns were famous for their birch, spruce, and sassafras beer, boiled with a fantastic variety of roots and herbs, spruce and sassafras bark, pumpkin and apple parings, molasses, maple syrup, beet tops, and other ingredients. As one New Englander bragged:

Oh, we can make liquor to sweeten our lips
Of pumpkins, of parsnips, or walnut-tree chips.

Virginians in 1725 quaffed a full-bodied Bristol malt beer supposedly made "exceedingly fine and smooth by having been tossed on ocean waves" during the long journey across the Atlantic.

As soon as the British occupied New York, they set up their own brewery "using only the best English malt" and selling only to "good, loyal men, true to their King and Parliament."

Malt was brewed in every colonial household. It was done by women. Gervase Markham wrote in his *Instructions to a Good Housewife:* "It is properly the work and care of a woman, for it is a housework. The man ought only to bring in and to provide the grain."

Colonial dames were not dainty. The frontier, especially, brought forth bold women who could hold their own against men, in drinking and all else. It was said that an American lady "could fight a rattlesnake and give it the two first bites." Indeed, Anne Blair of Williamsburg gave a lively account of a farting contest between two Virginia gentlewomen of distinction.

The oldest business in America may be the Francis Perot's Sons Malting Company in Philadelphia, founded by one Anthony Morris, born in London in 1654. He set up his Malt House and Brewery in Philadelphia on Front Street, in 1687, only 5 years after the founding of the city.

Two undainty dames from colonial days

George Washington maintained a small brewery on his estate.

Thomas Jefferson brewed a little "small drink" on his plantation. He was always on the lookout for good brewers and sponsored two beer makers from Bohemia to set up business in the colonies. Of a certain Captain Miller, asking permission to set up a brewery in Virginia, Jefferson said, "He is about to settle in this country and to establish a brewery, in which art I think him as skillful a man as has ever come to America."

Beer was such a huge success in the colonies because it was thought that water caused innumerable sicknesses, while beer and ale were wholesome and contained many curative powers.

Beer and ale were promoted in the colonies to foster abstinence on the theory that a man with a belly full of beer had no room to spare for "hot, hellish rum."

Among other famous brewers of ale and beer were Governor Oglethorpe, who established the colony of Georgia; Patrick Henry, who at one time tended bar in his uncle's tavern; Thomas Chittenden, first governor of Vermont and tavern keeper, whose strong beer was very popular; General Israel Putnam, Revolutionary War hero, who not only brewed beer, but also kept a tavern; John Hancock; Benjamin Rush, Washington's physician general and a signer of the Declaration of Independence; and Matthew Vassar, whose famous Vassar beer earned money enough to found the college of the same name.

Franklin, Hancock, and Jefferson pushed American beer because it hurt the British, put money into American pockets, and prevented addiction to stronger waters.

Jefferson once held up a glass of beer to his guests, saying, "I wish to see this beverage become common."

Prices for beer were fixed early. In 1634 the Massachusetts court set the price at "not above one penny for an ale-quart of beer."

The president of Harvard College urged the court to give a license to "Sister Bradish" (Brady), that she might be "encouraged and countenanced" in making bread and brewing beer at one penny a quart. He vowed that "such is her art, way, and skill that shee doth vend such comfortable penniworths for the relief of all that send unto her as elsewhere they can seldom meet with." "Comfortable penniworths" meant extralarge ones.

In 1850 the total U.S. output of alcoholic malt beverages—beer and ale—was 36,678,444 gallons, or 1.4 gallons per capita (including babies). In 1860 comsumption had tripled to 102,956,441 gallons, or 3.25 gallons per capita. Three years later it was over 500 million gallons, or 10 gallons per head.

The beer that conquered 19th-century America was German-type lager beer. *Lager* or *lagern* means "storing" or "keeping." Americans developed a taste for a light-bodied beer that could be chilled and swallowed in a hurry. The older, heavier beers did not take well to chilling and were too strong to be gulped down.

A German by the name of Wagner set up the first lager-beer brewery in a small stone building on the outskirts of Philadelphia in 1842.

By 1880 beer brewing was the chief industry of Milwaukee. In St. Louis and Cincinnati it was the second largest business.

Adolphus Busch came to St. Louis as a German immigrant shortly before the Civil War. He married the daughter of a brewery owner named Eberhard Anheuser. The result was the famous firm Anheuser-Busch. Adolphus built himself a medieval-style chateau on the brewery grounds and lived in a baronial manner. He was a friend of President Taft, who called him Prince Busch. His funeral in 1913 was the biggest ever in the Gateway City. He was buried in a German-made coffin weighing 800 pounds.

As Busch was the prince of St. Louis, so Captain Fred Pabst was the king of Milwaukee. He once bragged to an interviewer that any of the boys in his plant could down a large fire bucket full of foaming Pabst at one swallow. A malt master by the name of Otto was selected to make good Captain Fred's boast. "Just a moment," said Otto, and disappeared. He returned shortly and then accomplished the feat. "Why did you go out first?" inquired Pabst. "I didn't know if I could manage it," replied Otto, "so I tried it outside first."

HOPS ACROSS THE SEA

In 19th-century America going for a beer was called "rushing the growler." Beer was sold from kegs that were handled by "schooner skippers." They served "high-collared beer" in scuttles or schooners. A scuttle held about 3 normal bottles of beer. For three generations its price—1 nickel—remained unchanged.

In the low dens of the Bowery in New York, tipplers could get a swallow of beer for a penny. A hose was connected to each keg of beer, and the customer, after putting down one cent, could suck up as much of the brew as he was able to *without catching his breath.* Once he inhaled, the hose was yanked from his mouth. Chiselers who tried to cheat got the bum's rush. Some guzzlers learned to hold their breath for 2 minutes while sucking.

Up to 1934 75 percent of all beer consumed in America was "on tap"—that is, draught beer. By 1937 only 56 percent was draught (draft). In 1944 the first can of beer made its commerical appearance, to the joy of some and the sorrow of others.

After the repeal of Prohibition, beer came back with a vengeance among U.S. drinkers. In the first postrepeal year, some 25 million barrels of malt beverages were consumed. In 1965 consumption passed the 100 million mark. Since then it has almost doubled. Anheuser-Busch of St. Louis, the largest brewery in the world, sells close to 42 million barrels of beer a year. Americans drink beer at the rate of some 20 gallons per head per annum.

ABSOLUTELY **ALONE** AT THE TOP

of the world's bottled beers is the supreme position occupied by ***Old Reliable***

Budweiser

Its high reputation is due to its exclusive Saazer Hop flavor, its low percentage of alcohol and thorough ageing in the largest storage cellars in the world. Only the very best materials find their way into our plant.

Bottled only *(with corks or crown caps)* at the

Anheuser-Busch Brewery
St. Louis, Mo.

The largest breweries in the United States are, in order: (1) Anheuser-Busch, (2) Miller, (3) Pabst, and (4) Schlitz.

Wisconsin citizens quaff the greatest amount of malted beverages in the United States—26 gallons per capita per year. Alabamans are at the bottom of the list—barely 5 gallons per person (but they are far ahead of Wisconsin when it comes to bourbon).

The inhabitants of Australia manage to demolish beer to the tune of 62 U.S. gallons per head—women, the infirm, and infants included. It must be remembered that much of their habitat is hot and desertlike.

West Germans take the cake for beer consumption in temperate climes—40 gallons per person per annum.

DUCK THE DRUNKARD: Rum and religion in Early America

The Puritans enjoyed initialing vices: D *is for drunkenness.*

In spite of the fact that drinking in old New England was one of the few things that was not a sin, "swinish drunkenness," which led to rambunctiousness and disrespect toward authority, was frowned upon and punished.

For drunkenness men and women were whipped behind the cart, put in bilboes or stocks, stood in the pillory to be pelted with cow and horse dung, wore the red letter *D* (for "Drunkard") on their breast or sleeve, wore placards reading "Drunkard" around their necks, and, in cases of repeated violations, had their ears nailed to a tree or post.

The Pilgrims first punished an Indian for drunkenness in 1621.

In 1625 Thomas Morton, with a group of immigrants from the ship *Unity*, founded the village of Maremont, brewed a barrel of beer to be drunk "with all good cheare," set up a Maypole, and invited all and sundry, including indentured bondmen and Indians, to come and celebrate. This did not sit well with the worthies at Plymouth, who called Maremont "merrie Mont," the Maypole a filthy "idle" or "Idoll," and Morton's celebration beastly "dancing and frisking together like so many furies, or fairies, and worse practices." Poor Morton, after various scuffles, was "laid low by his heels" with bilboes—that is, was shackled—as an example to others.

In 1656 a certain Captain Kemble for "lewd and unseemly behavior kissing his wife publicquely on the Sabbath Day" was put in the stocks for 2 hours. The lewd kiss occurred just when the poor mariner returned after a 3-year voyage. The captain was not in the least reproved, however, for having a goodly supply of strong comfortables in the hold of his vessel.

Gibbets, stocks, and pillories were always set up conveniently before a public house for the amusement and edification of the guests:

Cambridge is a famous town,
Both for wit and knowledge,
Some they whip and some they hang,
And some they send to college.

As Sam Johnson said to a Quaker lady, "Madam, we have different modes of restraining evil—stocks for men, a ducking stool for women, and a pound for beasts." The ducking stool was invented especially to punish women. There is no record of it being used on a man. The stool was the punishment mainly for using a sharp tongue against one's husband, slandering one's betters, or talking back to

magistrates, but it was also employed to "subdue bould virgins" who inveigled their swains to kiss them, or who were found tippling. Here again, it was perfectly all right for a fine lady to punish a bottle of Rhenish or claret in her home, but most unseemly for the servant girl to have a dram of the vile stuff in public.

The usual punishment for disobedience to one's husband, strong verbal abuse in public, and drunkenness was being ducked 5 times for half a minute each. The last ducking on record took place in 1811.

THE CRADLE OF LIBERTIE: The role of booze in the Revolutionary War

The colonial tavern and dramshop has been called "the cradle of libertie in which the cock-a-doodle-doo, the rooster crow of Democracy, was heard for the first time." It was in the old ordinaries and tippling houses that rebellion was hatched and plans made. It was in taverns that the Sons of Liberty met and the Minutemen assembled and did their drinking.

On August 14, 1769, American patriots crowded into Boston's Liberty Tree Tavern to protest the Stamp Act. They downed 14 bottoms-up toasts to liberty and then trooped to Dorchester, where they drank 45 more. The Sons of Liberty's enthusiasm for fighting parliamentary tyranny was limitless.

At the Eagle Tavern in the Green Mountains, militia captain William Watson offered his famous toast: "The enemies of our country! May they have cobweb breeches, a porcupine saddle, a hard trotting horse, and an eternal journey!"

The Liberty Tree Tavern was named after the famous elm that stood before it, to which was attached an iron plaque with the legend "This tree was planted in 1646, and pruned by order of the Sons of Liberty February 14, 1766." A company of lobsterbacks cut down the tree, which supplied them with 14 cords of firewood.

Daniel Webster called the Green Dragon Tavern the "Headquarters of the Revolution." In its taproom the Boston Tea Party was planned, and in its chambers patriots disguised themselves as Indians to carry out the plan.

Paul Revere wrote, "In the fall of 1774 and winter of 1775, I was one of upwards of thirty men, chiefly mechanics, who formed ourselves with a Committee for the purpose of watching the British soldiers and gaining every intelligence of the movement of the Tories. We held our meetings at the Green Dragon Tavern."

The Wright House in Concord, Massachusetts, had been opened by militia captain Ephraim Jones in 1741. It was in this tavern that the British Major Pitcairn stirred his brandy with a cut, bleeding thumb, vowing to "stir the Yankee blood this day!"

Major Pitcairn cauterizing one of the war's first wounds

It was in the Buckman Tavern at Lexington where, on a raw April morning, the Minutemen drank their hot toddies and mugs of flip before going outside to "fire the shot heard round the world." The tavern walls contain many British musket balls.

It was in front of the Royal Exchange, headquarters for British officers, that the Boston Massacre occurred and the first blood of the Revolution was shed. The tavern can be seen in the background of Paul Revere's famous woodcut depicting the event.

In 1775 the U.S. Marine Corps was founded inside Philadelphia's Tun Tavern.

Around a table in Rhode Island's Red Sabin Tavern, patriots planned the capture of the British schooner *Gaspee*, which interfered with their rumrunning. And at the Red Sabin they assembled, their innards warmed with Hot Buttered Rum, to realize their plans.

It is said that Paul Revere did not gallop forth with the cry "The redcoats are coming!" until he had fortified himself with a flagon of extraordinarily fine Medford rum.

Thomas Jefferson wrote the Declaration of Independence inside Philadelphia's Indian Queen while sampling the tavern's famous beer.

Francis Scott Key worked on his "Star Spangled Banner" in Baltimore's Fountain Inn.

Patrick Henry plotted rebellion while tending bar in his father-in-law's taproom at Hanover Courthouse.

On May 5, 1775, in Steven Fay's Catamount Tavern, at Bennington, Prudence Fay was serving Stone Walls to the boys. Stone Walls were a specialty of the house, a hellish mixture of rum and especially hard applejohn. The "boys" consisted of Ethan Allen, Remember Baker, Seth Hall, and a goodly number of Green Mountain Boys.

Nursing their Stone Walls, appropriately served in stone mugs, they discussed recent events—Concord and Lexington. As the fiery liquor inflamed their minds, the boys grew belligerent. Some progressed from Stone Walls to Flap Dragons, Allen pouring alcohol over beer, lighting it, and downing it—flames and all. By then the boys were rollicking drunk. "By the Great Jehosaphat!" roared Allen, "let's take Ticonderoga!"

According to the legend, the Green Mountain Boys uprooted the Catamount's sign, a stuffed snarling mountain lion, and carried it

The inspired Green Mountain Boys with their feline mascot

triumphantly before them as their flag. They stopped at every grogshop on the way, switching to straight rum and brandy, gathering up men as they went along. They took Fort Ti by surprise, Allen roaring, "Come on out there, you British sons of bitches!" Out came a yawning Captain Delaplace in his nightshirt, together with his mistress, also in dishabille, surrendering fort and garrison and inviting Allen to try his most precious Madeira. The Green Mountain Boys, disdaining sissified drinks, helped themselves to the garrison's rum supply, managing to drink up 90 gallons of the stuff. They would have drunk more had there been any left. Ninety gallons of rum, 83 Green Mountain Boys, and then they started working on the small supply of wine and Madeira—in desperation, one supposes. Of course, they had not been quite sober when they found the rum. Thus Ethan Allen conquered Ticonderoga "in the name of the Great Lord God Jehovah and the Continental Congress."

The British put a price on Allen's head, "dead or alive." Ethan rode into Albany, went into a tavern, drank 2 large bowls of punch, faced the crowd, and exclaimed: "Now, then, my name is Allen. Who wants that reward?"

Old Put's tavern sign.

General Israel Putnam—"Old Put"—was a colorful character. During the war he escorted pretty Mistress Bush from Cos Cob to a dance at the Israel Knapp Tavern in Greenwich, Connecticut. Retiring in the small hours of the morning and sleeping late, he was only half shaved when told that the British were upon him. He jumped on his horse, half of his face still covered with thick lather, saving himself by a madcap ride through woods and over precipices. After the War of the Revolution, Old Put went back to his old job, brewing beer and tending the General Wolfe Tavern at Brooklyn, Connecticut.

According to one Englishman, more than one third of the American general officers "have been inn-keepers, and have been chiefly indebted to that circumstance for such rank."

After the final victory, a great celebration was held at Black Sam Fraunces's tavern, with Washington as the guest of honor. Thirteen toasts were drunk from large tumblers—one for each state of the young republic. Washington overslept the next morning.

Fraunces Tavern in 1854

It was in Boston's Green Dragon Inn that the city's mechanics voted, by acclamation, to urge the adoption of the Constitution by the federal convention. Commented Samuel Adams, "Well, if they want it they must have it."

HERRING JUICE, HENBANE, AND HEMLOCK:
Incidentals in the world of beer

Anheuser-Busch and Pabst experimented with cans as early as 1929. In 1933 the Gottfried Krueger Brewing Company of Newark put beer into cans and in 1935 began selling canned brew.

The earliest beer cans were made of steel. Aluminum came into use after World War II. Having beer in cans made it easy to ship the stuff to G.I.s overseas.

At first, cans came with a cone-shaped top. This made them look more like bottles, which was desirable in breaking down the public's initial resistance to canned beer. Some cans came with handles to make them look like mugs.

Beer cans come in all shapes and sizes, as well as in myriad different designs. The Germans manufactured enormous cans, shaped like barrels and holding no less than 5 liters of beer.

The Simonds Brewery put its Half Yard of Tavern brand of beer in—you guessed it—a half-yard-long can.

A special beer can was designed for Princeton University students.

A beer-can fancier is called a canologist.

Beer-can collecting is the world's fastest-growing hobby. There are, at the moment, some 80,000 collectors in the United States, Canada, England, Europe, and Japan. Some 15,000 belong to B.C.C.A.—Beer Can Collectors of America. Their motto is "Don't Kick the Can." Their meetings are called "canventions."

Rare beer cans fetch lofty prices. A temporary can issued by Tennent's in Glasgow during a shortage of their regular cans sells for $150 or more. A can of Mellow Yellow fetches between $300 and $400. Cans featuring *Playboy* Playmates go for $500 a pair. (They are rare because Hugh Hefner of *Playboy* sued the brewer for using his little rabbits without permission, and the cans had to be withdrawn.) A set of James Bond's 007 cans sells for $2,500.

The strongest beer sold in the United States—the beer with the highest alcoholic content—is Kulmbacher, a dark-brown Bavarian brew with over 13 percent alcohol.

Among the weakest beers in the United States are "near" beers, such as are sold in Kansas. Some of these have less than 2 percent alcohol.

The weakest beer on record was the German Marschall Hindenburg's Kriegs Bier, a World War I ersatz brew with about 1 percent alcohol. It was made mostly from a weed called *Sauerampfer.*

Steam beer is an American oddity, brewed in small quantities in California for connoisseurs who enjoy its "bubbliness," caused by a high content of carbon dioxide gas. It was invented in 1850 to furnish brew to hardy goldminers. As ice was not available to ferment beer at the usual low temperature, the brewers invented a process for manufacturing beer at comparatively high temperatures. The result was steam beer.

Bock beer simply means "billy goat beer," hence the picture of a goat's head on many bock-beer labels. It was first brewed during the Middle Ages in the city of Einbeck near Hamburg. *Einbeck* was mistaken for *Ein Bock* ("a billy goat"), and thus the name was born. Bock is heavy and tasty, with a slightly sweet malt flavor.

On the day Prohibition ended, the jubilant cry was "Bock is back!"

Beer has always been called "the wholesome brew." It is therefore not to be wondered at that it was used as medicine. In Georgetown, Colorado, the Red Ram Saloon advertised "Selak's celebrated ale, takes right hold of the vitals and elevates the soul. It opens the faculties, clears the canals of the heart, and strikes down to the very bottom of contentedness." It sold for a nickel per mug.

In 1598 an English savant named William Vaugh asserted, "Stale beere, with a good store of sugar, eyther in the morning, or before meales, it rejoiceth the heart, cleareth the complexion, and cureth melancholy."

Ale: It'll put new feathers on your chest.

Toward the end of the 17th century, a London quack named Moses Springer claimed to have a secret remedy, mixed with ale and beer, that would restore youth and sexual vigor to the aged. Speaking of himself in the third person, he wrote: "That learned Chymist made his first experiment upon a Hen, so very old that nobody would kill it. He mingled some of his medicine, which he called Renovating Quintessence (also "Elixir Renovans"), with a quantity of Barly and gave it to the Hen. The effects were wonderful, and the Hen recovered Youth and New Feathers, LAID eggs, and HATCHT chickens as if she had lost a dozen years of her age." Springer then claimed to rejuvenate humans, among them an "Ancient Woman upon the very margin of death," who recovered health, youth, teeth, and hair, became amorous, and started to menstruate again.

A doctor named Solas Dodd used a concoction of warm ale, herring juice, wild boar's gall, catnip, henbane, and hemlock to render patients "insensible." Having drunk this wondrous ale, they could be operated on "without feelinge the slightest inconvenience."

Warm ale with an infusion of wormwood was considered a "Sovereign Remedie for the Hiccops."

In taverns called The Cock, a strange beverage was sold, very popular until well into the 18th century. This was Cock-ale. It consisted of the body of an unfortunate rooster, dissolved in a keg of ale together with a great number of other ingredients, such as raisins, rosemary, mace, cayenne, dates, and honey. When the brew was ready, a bottle of Madeira was poured into it for that special last touch. Cock-ale was supposed to be a royal cure for dropsy, consumption, whooping cough, colic, the bloody flux, and—last but not least—worms.

The words *herbal* and *herbalist* come from "herb ale," strong, warm ale mixed with medicinal herbs and taken as a cure.

A 17th-century fisherman, Harry Jenkins, credited his longevity to his daily gallon of strong ale. He supposedly died at the age of 165.

A study made in England concluded that rinsing teeth with beer prevents cavities.

THE KING OF SMALL DRINK: Cider

Johnny Appleseed, who sowed seeds for more than 4 decades

Cider is one of the oldest alcoholic beverages known. Its name stems from the Hebrew *shakar* or *shekar* mentioned in the Bible, a word meaning "strong drink." *Shikker* is still the Yiddish word for being drunk. The Greeks transformed this into *sikera*—whence *cider.*

Sweet cider has a low alcoholic content, 3 to 4 percent by volume, and sparkling champagne cider has about 7 percent. Applejack, hard cider, and Jersey Lightning, however, are fierce indeed—as high in alcoholic content, sometimes, as whiskey or vodka.

Pliny the Elder spoke of wine made from apples. St. Augustine stated that the Manichaeans drank a delicious liquor made from apple juice. The Roman theologian Tertullian also mentioned a beverage pressed from apples, which he described as strong and vinous. St. Jerome mentions a fermented apple juice drink called *sicera.*

Cider was made by Gauls and Britons from wild apples growing in the forests—from crab apples.

Around A.D. 800 Charlemagne made laws to protect and further the manufacture of cider. He himself was very fond of the stuff.

Cider was drunk instead of wine during the Hundred Years' War, from the mid-14th century to the mid-15th, by English citizens not able to procure wine from France.

It was forbidden by the English church to baptize infants with cider.

In Merry Old England, farmhands often received part of their wages in "scrumpy"—that is, homemade cider.

In 1573 a certain Sieur de Gaulmier wrote the definitive book on cider, the *Traité du Sidre.* He maintained that apples fitting to be pressed into cider were introduced into France by Señor Dursus from Spain in A.D. 1486.

France, *la patrie du vin,* produces more cider than wine.

A person with scientific knowledge of apples is called a *pomologist* (*ponum, poma,* is Latin for "fruit," and *pomme* is French for "apple").

John, first viscount of Scudamore, has been called the "Father of British Cider." In the 17th century, during the so-called Restoration period, he developed on his Hereford estates some 300 varieties of apples suitable for cider making, including the famous Red Streak apple—the "foundation apple" upon which modern English cider making rests.

H. P. Bulmer, founded in 1884, purveyors to the royal cellar, is the greatest commercial cider company in the world today. Its gigantic storage vat, the biggest in the world, holds 1.65 million gallons of cider.

By the year 1700 cider in various forms had replaced beer and ale as the common beverage in English-speaking North America.

Apples were not native to the New World. In North America there was a variety of wild crab apple, more or less unfit for human consumption. There is no evidence that Indians ever made cider.

Apples were first cultivated in America in the year 1626, in Massachusetts Bay Colony, from English seeds.

Governor's Island was given to John Winthrop by the Massachusetts Bay Company on condition that he plant an apple orchard on it.

Apple trees grow fast. Under favorable conditions, a person can plant the scions and have the first apples 6 years later.

In 1638 there was an apple orchard at the foot of what is now Beacon Hill in Boston. The apples weren't eaten; they all went into cider.

In 1689 applejack was first made in New Jersey—the state soon became the nation's foremost source for fermented apple beverages.

New York was famous for its finely cared-for orchards at a very early date. Favorite varieties were Poughkeepsie Swaar, Kingston Spitzenburg, Newton Pippin, and Guelderleng. Some of the names for various kinds of apples were quite poetic: Golden Sweet, Lyman's Pumpkin Sweet, Belle-Fleur, Sweet Paradise, William's Favorite, Cloth of Gold, Maiden's Blush, Belle et Bonne, Peck's Pleasant, and Seek-No-Further.

Henry Ward Beecher's pet apple varieties were Lady's Flesh and Love's Pear, surprising choices for a divine.

Today there are between 5,000 and 6,000 varieties of apples grown in the United States.

Lovers of good cider owe a debt of gratitude to Johnny Appleseed (John Chapman), who was born in Springfield, Massachusetts, in 1774. In 1801 he set out for the West, planting apple seeds along his path. He walked barefoot, summer and winter, and wore a tin pan instead of a hat (he used the pan to do his cooking). He often retraced his steps to see how his little apple trees were doing. Indians did not harm him, because they thought him mad and madness was holy. When Johnny died in Indiana at the age of 72, he had planted apple seeds over an area of more than 100,000 square miles.

Cider was the cheapest drink in early New England. The more apple trees that became mature, the cheaper the price became.

A pilgrim named Josselyn reported in 1670, "I have had at the tap-houses of Boston an ale-quart of cider, spiced and sweetened with sugar, for a groat." A groat was less than a penny. Cider was cheaper than beer.

Laborers were always furnished generous amounts of the exhilarating drink. It was said that the making of a New England stone wall progressed at the rate of 1 gallon of cider per rod.

One of the most potent colonial drinks was a mixture of cider and rum. It was called a Stone Wall.

No colonial court of justice would sit without a plentiful supply of cider, sweet and hard, for judge, jurors, and defendants.

Condemned criminals were mercifully given a gallon of hard Jersey cider or applejack to steady them for the trip to the gallows. Nor was the hangman forgotten.

Cider was used to pay the rent in early America and was also bequeathed to one's descendants. One Alexander Moore of New York left his widow 20 gallons of raw cider and 130 of boiled.

Cider was served up automatically to the students of Yale and Harvard at dinner, being passed in 2-quart tankards from student to student down the common table.

Old and infirm persons were advised to start the day with a quart or two of hard cider before breakfast as a lift to a sagging constitution, and the oldsters took the advice.

Delicate expecting mothers drank cider for strength and easy childbirth.

Cider reached the acme of popularity during the 1840 presidential "Log Cabin and Cider" campaign. To remind the common man that the Whig candidates, William Henry Harrison ("Old Tippecanoe") and John Tyler, had been born "just plain folks," a log cabin and a cider barrel were chosen as their symbols. During the campaign, hard cider was ladled out free to all who were either old enough to vote or looked like it. Old Tippecanoe won handily.

The apple crop was so wholly used to make cider that at the beginning of the great temperance movement members of the pro-prohibition Washington Society invaded New England to cut down fruit-bearing trees, not imagining that apples could be used for anything but cider making.

In 1721 one Massachusetts village of 40 families manufactured 3,000 barrels of cider.

In 1728 Joseph Wilder, a judge of Lancaster, Massachusetts, wrote down with some satisfaction that he had made 616 barrels of cider that year. "Drunk as a judge" was one of the earliest colonial sayings ("Sober as a judge" came much later on, during the Victorian age).

According to one statistic, 18th-century ministers on the average stored 40 barrels of cider each for their winter use. (New England winters are notoriously long.)

President John Adams remarked that "If the ancients drank wine as our people drink rum and cider, it is no wonder we hear of so many possessed with devils." Adams himself always started his day with a large tankard of hard cider before breakfast, keeping up the habit until he died at age 91.

In the year 1767 the good citizens of Massachusetts demolished cider at the rate of 1.14 barrels per capita.

Cider spirits were called "gumption"—hence a man was said to have gumption, to be tough and strong like the essence of applejack.

The Reverend Edward Holyoke, sometime president of Harvard, always laid in 30 barrels of cider, fortifying each further with a bottle of fiery rum. His son, Augustus, Harvard's first graduate in medicine, also mixed his hard cider with rum and took half a pint at breakfast, half a pint at dinner, and a further half pint as a nightcap with his smoke. He lived to be 100 and celebrated his own centennial with his usual libations and a spirited toast.

The forefathers had a thirst "five fathoms deep." The eye opener that helped them start the day was only the beginning. Drinking continued throughout the day and until bedtime. This resulted not infrequently in tipsiness:

You're a purty man!—you air!
With a pair o' eyes like two fried eggs
An' a nose like a Bartlutt Pear!

One great favorite of Philadelphians was Stewed Quaker, a mug of hard cider in which a hot baked apple had been immersed. It was related that the ladies of refinement were so enamored of Stewed Quaker that they became "haily-gaily."

Scotchem was a concoction of applejack, boiling water, and a more than generous dash of hot ground mustard. A trapper who tried it coughed, with tears streaming down his cheeks, and managed to stammer bravely, "It's good, an' it's tasty, too, ef it does favor tomato ketchup."

Metheglin was a favorite drink of the American colonists. It was imbibed by Kentuckians until well into the 20th century. Half hard and half soft, it was made from a mixture of cider, honey, and a sort of gall-apple made by the kermes insect.

According to Alice Morse Earle: "Bradford tells of backsliders from Merrymont who 'abased themselves disorderly with drinking too much stronge drinke aboard the Freindshipp.'" This strong drink was metheglin, of which two hogsheads were to be delivered at Plymouth. But after it was transferred to wooden "flackets" in Boston, these *Friendship* merrymakers contrived to "drinke it up under the name 'leakage' till but six gallons of the metheglin arrived at Plymouth."

"Your're a purty man!—you air!"

An exceedingly strong drink was Cider Royal, made by boiling 4 barrels of ordinary applejack down into 1 barrel of the supremely potent royal stuff. In Philadelphia, at the Red Lion Tavern on Elbow Lane in the year 1736, one Thomas Apty "laid a wager of Half a Crown that he could drink within the space of one hour and a half, a Gallon of Cyder Royall, which he had no sooner accomplished and said, 'I have finished,' but he fell down and then expired."

In 1633 the men of New Hampshire made a list of values they set on furs, the legal tender of the colony at the time for want of hard money, making "6 Gallon Mathaglin worth 2 Lb Beaver."

Perry and Peachie were the names of drinks made from fermented or distilled pears and peaches. Virginia Drams was a favorite kind of Peachie.

Taverns made their own brands of cider, hard and soft, and some of these became known far and wide, such as Moral Suasion, Ne Plus Ultra, Deacon, and Sweet Ruination.

New Jersey White Lightning was so hard that a piece of hog fat thrown into it completely dissolved within half an hour. It often gave imbibers a bad case of "apple palsies."

A merrymaker, quite haily-gaily, rolling on home.

THE BLOOD OF THE GODS: The history of wine

"Here's looking at you!"

Wine is almost as old as beer—in the opinion of some archaeologists, even older. Some say that cavemen, after a successful mammoth hunt, refreshed themselves with wine made from fermented wild honey.

In Mesopotamia the earliest wine was probably palm wine. Early Greek travelers said that it gave one a tremendous hangover. In the 4th century B.C., Xenophon in his *Anabasis* writes that palm wine was "sweet, but headachy." He was talking from experience.

Grape wine was first made in Persia, the modern Iran. In the Iran of today, in obedience to Koranic law, the drinking of wine and all alcoholic beverages is strictly forbidden and severely punished.

In many ancient religions, and some not so ancient ones, wine often represented the blood of the god(s). Indeed, wine drinking was at first a religious ritual.

Toasts seem to have been invented by the Mesopotamians of old. Bas-reliefs show stiff, unsmiling Assyrian courtiers, with carefully curled beards and hair, gravely pledging each other with ornamental cups.

Egyptian wine grapes were grown in arbors on trellises, as shown in many ancient paintings. In time, pharaohs became connoisseurs of good wine. In Tutankhamen's grave, each wine jar bore a seal and inscription specifying vintage, locality, and the grower's name. Thus: "Year 4. Wine from the House of Aton on the Western River. Chief vintner Nen."

Some pharaohs got as thoroughly soused as common laborers. Of the 6th-century B.C. King Amasis it is said that he was inordinately partial to an intoxicating drink called *Kelebi.* He told his courtiers, "It is my lordly pleasure to drink good Egyptian Kelebi." The courtiers lamented, "Oh, great Lord, it is hard for us to drink Kelebi." (They did not have their master's capacity.) Amasis said,

"Do ye not like that which I am telling you?" They answered, "Oh, our mighty Lord, that which pleases pharaoh, let him do." Amasis did. The next morning the king "could not rise due to a certain heaviness in his limbs." The sun reached its zenith, but still the mighty lord could not get up. The courtiers lamented, "How can such things be? How can the Land of the Two Rivers be ruled?"

The great king Amasis doing that which pleased him

Wine is mentioned 521 times in the Bible. St. Paul the Apostle advised, "Drink no longer water but use a little wine for thy stomach's sake and thine often infirmities."

Noah is credited with being the primal vintner. The first thing he did after the deluge was plant a vineyard. As a result he got very drunk. (Gen. 9:20–21)

The servants of Absalom slew Amnon when his heart was "merry with wine." When drinking himself drunk, Elah was murdered by his servant Zimri. Ahab, on the advice of the prophet, surprised and defeated Benhadad, king of Syria, whom he found with 32 kings "drinking themselves drunk in the pavilions."

Isaiah 24:11 says, "There is a crying for wine in the streets, the lack of which takes all joy of life away."

Ecclesiastes enjoins us to "Eat thy bread with joy, and drink thy wine with a merry heart."

Caleb and Joshua returning with the grapes, Numbers 21:23

Christ's first miracle occurred when, at the marriage of Cana, he changed water into wine.

When the ancient biblical city of Gideon in Palestine was excavated, the remains of a huge commercial winery were unearthed. They contained a number of very large wine presses of stone in which grapes had been crushed.

The Scythians were thought to be the greatest winebibbers of antiquity. "To drink like a Scythian" was a byword.

Phoenician sailors and merchants brought the first grapevines to Greece in the 7th century B.C. The vines were quickly cultivated.

According to legend, it was the god Dionysus (Bacchus) who fled from Asia to Greece, bringing the heavenly drink to the Hellenes. He could not stand the ale-drinking Asiatics, it was said.

Dionysus introduced the orgy, ecstasy, enthusiasm, and holy frenzy. It was women who first took to the new religion. As bacchantes and maenads, they drank great quantities of the godly liquid, mixed with milk and honey. Hot with wine, dancing to the throb of the tympanum, they tore living animals apart, eating their flesh raw. They also raped men who got in their way.

The Greeks usually mixed their wine with water—some say because early Greek wines were unpalatable when taken neat. Others says they diluted their drinks out of a natural love for moderation.

On thousands of ancient Greek vases, drunkards are depicted throwing up, staggering home supported by friends, or having their heads held by comforting females. Another favorite artistic motif is drunken satyrs with huge erections pursuing maenads, who are casting back come-hither looks.

In 415 B.C., on a drunken nocturnal spree, the Athenian general and statesman Alcibiades and some friends knocked off the phalli of Athens's Hermes stele (these were a sort of statue consisting of a stone slab with a carved head and penis). This was sacrilege, punishable by death. Alcibiades, who had been named commander-in-chief for the Sicilian expedition, had to flee. Less talented

A moment of tender Greek intimacy

generals were appointed in his stead and made a mess of it. Eventually Athens was conquered by Sparta. If Alcibiades had not gotten drunk . . .

In the 16th century, a Japanese generalissimo, Oda Nobunaga, had a few sakes too many under his kimono. He used his fan to drum a merry tune on the bald head of his chief general, one Akechi Mitsuhide. The insulted Mitsuhide seized the first opportunity to assassinate Nobunaga, giving Japanese history a new twist.

Alexander the Great, no teetotaler he, slew his general and closest friend Clitus, pinning him to a wall with his spear. They were both very drunk, and Clitus had made a disrespectful remark. At the battle of the Granicus in 334 B.C., Clitus had saved Alexander's life. Alexander was very sorry about killing Clitus when he sobered up.

Alexander the Great was an alcoholic. He may have become addicted to wine under the influence of his father, King Philip II of Macedon, also a heavy drinker. During one drinking bout, Alexander threw his wine cup at the head of a certain Attalus. The enraged Philip threatened his son with a sword, but then fell flat on his face. Alexander cried, "Men of Macedon, see here the man who was preparing to pass from Europe into Asia! He is so drunk he cannot even pass from one table to another!"

A woman once brought a law case to Philip for decision. Philip ruled against her. The woman said, "I appeal!" "How?" asked Philip. "From your king, to whom then?" "To Philip, when sober," was the spirited reply. The king thought for a while and then decided in the woman's favor.

Alexander the Great's mother was a devotee of the Dionysus cult.

Alexander came to an untimely end due to overindulgence. Lying in bed, sick with fever, he got into a health-drinking contest with a certain Proteas, matching him cup for cup. When he had swallowed about 16 quarts, the cup fell from his hand and he himself fell back dead. He had had one cup too many of the so-called Cup of Hercules, a drinking vessel of outlandish proportions.

Symposium is the Greek term for "drinking together." At a symposium the guests elected a leader, who decided whether to drink the wine neat or mixed, whether to drink little or much. Myrtle twigs were handed around. Whoever got one had to sing a *skolion*, or drinking song.

At drinking parties philosophers discussed the nature of the universe, the meaning of life, and love. More often dancing girls, female flutists, and acrobats amused the symposiasts, bestowing sexual favors upon the guests for a price.

Komos is the word for what happened after a symposium. Komos was the practice of not going home after a drinking party, but rather wandering through the streets in a group, pausing before houses to serenade a pretty girl or a plump-bottomed boy, taking swigs from a wineskin, throwing up, or relieving an overflowing bladder against a convenient wall.

Imperial Rome adopted the practice of komos in a much coarser form. Nero and his drinking buddies beat up citizens for fun, did great damage to private property, and engaged in drunken brawls that endangered life and limb. Nero loved to push his companions into open sewer holes. At banquets he made his guests heavy with wine and then prevented them in various ways from urinating—to his amusement and their distress.

In Greece priests of Dionysus fared better than Nero's guests. At festivals they sat on special marble chairs. They had to partake of the god's blood—that is, drink plenty of wine. After that they had to stay put for hours watching a tragedy, not being allowed to leave their seats under any circumstances. However, for their convenience, a narrow drainage pipe was inconspicuously built into each seat so that by a hardly noticeable lifting of their tunics they could get rid of that which plagued them.

Pramnian wine is often mentioned by Homer. It was considered the best in the earliest days of ancient Greece. King Nestor served Pramnian to his guest Machaon from a huge four-handled cup that only the king himself could lift. In historic times, wine from the islands of Thasos, Chios, and Samos was highly prized. Chian wine was preferred above all others and exported to most of the countries of the ancient world. Judging from the great numbers of wine amphorae recovered from Greek vessels, wine must have been the Greeks' main export.

One old tale has it that the Athenians, carrying out a scorched-earth policy before the invading Persians, made their stores of wine unpalatable by putting resin from pine trees into it. The occupying Persian guardsmen fell upon the wine . . . and gagged. After the Persians retreated, the thirsty Athenians had only the resin wine to drink. Having stronger stomachs than the effeminate Persians, they got used to the taste and learned to like it. The modern wine Retsina is the result.

Greeks and Romans drank before-dinner wines infused with wormwood, seawater, asafoetida, myrrh, pepper, and tar.

Socrates said, "Wine moistens the soul and lulls our grief to sleep while it also awakens kindly feelings."

The Greek's attitude to wine is expressed by Aeschylus in one sentence: "Wine is the mirror of the heart."

The Greeks taught viniculture to the Etruscans, who passed the art on to the Romans.

The earliest Greek name for Italy was *Oenotria* ("the land of the vine").

During the times of the Romans the most highly esteemed Italian wines were grown south of Rome. Praenestre, Velitrae, and Formiae, cities in the Alban hills, were famous for their excellent wines. Fine wines also came from the slopes of Mount Vesuvius, and Caecuban wine from Terracina was pronounced by Emperor Augustus to be "the noblest of all."

The best Roman wines had the name of the current consul and his year of office inscribed on the seals of the jars.

Young Roman winemakers at work

Many Roman connoisseurs maintained that the best wine was Opimian, put in jars when Lucius Opimius was consul in 121 B.C. A century after Opimius's consulship, Opimian wine could be found only in the private cellars of the very rich, such as the multimillionaire Crassus.

Really first-class wines in Rome were hideously expensive. The poet Horace complained that his means did not allow him to purchase them.

Pliny the Elder, born A.D. 23, sampled 80 varieties of "really good wine" in his lifetime, two-thirds of them Italian.

Of all the many fine wines of ancient Rome, only one, Falernian, survived and is still drunk today. Martial called this wine "immortal." Horace called it "fiery." Cicero said that it should not bear the stamp of the consul currently in office, nor the stamp of the consul Annicius, who lived more than a hundred years before Cicero. In other words, Falernian should not be drunk when new, nor should it be too old. The wine was best when it was between 10 and 30 years old.

The Romans had a wine to which seawater had been added, together with pitch, rosin, and turpentine. An educated Greek traveler remarked that it needed getting used to.

Pliny the Elder complained, "Man is satisfied with nothing in the state he receives it from the hand of nature." Unfortunately, this included wine, and unscrupulous Roman vintners were not above doctoring their product.

Pliny the Elder also lamented the luxury of his fellow citizens who put snow in their wine.

How good the ancients were at judging the taste of wine remains debatable. They put pigeon droppings into it to strengthen the flavor and give it a kick.

Since the art of distillation was not known to the ancients, the masters of the Roman Empire had to do without the hard stuff. Besides wine, they had *mulsum*, made of four parts wine and one part honey. They also could enjoy a mixture called *mulsa*, made of fermented honey and water. For a while *picatum*, a wood-pitch-flavored import from Gaul, was the rage. It did not last. From Egypt came date and mulberry wine. Sweet liquors are mentioned, but the recipe has been lost. Good Italian wines were better than Greek wines and eventually displaced the latter. The writer Arrian vowed that good Roman *vinum* was appreciated in places as far away as India.

During the time of the kings and in the earliest days of the republic, Roman women were forbidden to drink wine on pain of death. Taking into their own bodies the blood of a male god was not only sacrilege, but also adultery, and punished as such. In the Roman household the father was the absolute ruler. He did not want women to run around in orgasmic drunkenness like Greek or Etruscan maenads. There was also the fact that the male chauvinist Roman men thought that wine was too good to waste on women.

At banquets of the nouveaux riches during the heyday of Rome, guests sampled a hundred dishes and almost as many wines. From time to time the guests would go outside, tickle their throats with a feather, throw up, and thus make room for more sampling.

Etruscans and Romans did their eating and drinking reclining on couches, that is, lying down. They considered this more comfortable than sitting up and also better for their digestion.

The saloons in ancient Rome were so numerous that Martial said the city was "one vast tavern."

In the days of the emperors, the symposium degenerated into the Roman *commissatio,* or drinking bout. At such affairs the throw of the dice determined who among the participants would act as the *rex* or *magister bibendi,* that is, master of revelries. The master decided how much wine each had to drink—regardless of taste or capacity. Guests proposed the health of anyone present, and the person so honored had to drain his bumper at one swallow. The result can be imagined. In the words of one historian, the revelers staggering home "made the night hideous."

Tricongius, or the "Three-Gallon Knight," was the nickname of a Roman of the equestrian order, Novellius Torquatus, who could drink 3 gallons of unmixed wine at a draught without taking a breath. Of Caius Piso it was said that he would go on drinking for 2 days and nights without interruption and without leaving the table. The almost 7-foot tall Emperor Maximin could drink 6 gallons of wine at a sitting.

One of the best-known Roman proverbs is *In vino veritas*—"There is truth in wine." Too much truth, sometimes, as not a few citizens who had talked loosely found out to their sorrow, particularly under the reigns of Tiberius and Caligula.

The Roman writer poet Avienus said, "Wine refreshes the spirits and is itself easily converted into them."

Perhaps the Romans' feeling about wine was best expressed in this ancient oath: "If I speak true, let my bowl always be filled with wine, but if I lie let it be filled with water."

THE WHORES OF VENICE AND THE WINES OF VICENZA: European wines

North of the ancient, wine-drinking civilizations, the earliest form of wine drunk was mead, also called "honey ale" or "honey wine."

Men and women collecting wild honey (probably for making mead) are depicted in Stone Age paintings and Egyptian tombs.

The ancient Irish called mead *miodh* and *mil'fion* ("honey wine").

The word *mead* is derived from the Indo-European *madhu,* the Chinese *myit,* the Slav *medhu,* and the Welsh *meddyglyn,* which meant either honeyed or spiced drink. Its main ingredients were fermented honey mixed with fermented grape juice.

Mead was held in such high respect in medieval England that at the court of the ancient princes of Wales, the mead maker was held as the eleventh person in rank and point of dignity.

The Nordic peoples had a legend according to which it was the god Odin who brought the gift of mead to mankind. There was a certain Kvaser, the wisest being that ever lived. Kvaser was already grown up when he was born. He knew how and when the world was made. Actually, the gods had formed Kvaser out of a huge jar that was always in their way, so that they stubbed their toes on it. One day Kvaser the Wise was walking through a forest and the two wicked dwarfs, Galar and Fjalar, killed him. They wanted his blood, which was very precious. They poured it into 3 enormous kettles and mixed it with honey. This was the first mead. The wicked dwarfs, however, had their comeuppance when they messed with a certain Suttung, the son of a giant. Suttung was about to kill them when they promised to give him the mead if he spared their lives. So Suttung, a giant himself, had the mead, the only mead in all the world. He built himself an underground hall, tunneling deep into the rock, and there he kept Kvaser's sweet, intoxicating blood, and let nobody near it. Now Odin disguised himself as a simple farmhand, going by the name of Bolverk, and spied out the lay of the land, or rather Suttung's underground cellar. There was only a small hole leading into it that was unguarded. Odin turned himself into a long, fat worm and wiggled his way into the mead cellar. The 3 huge kettles were watched by Suttung's daughter Gunlad, a comely wench. Odin immediately turned himself from a worm into a beautiful young man and charmed the tunic off Gunlad. "What he said to the maid, and what went on between them we know not," says the saga. A little while later Odin, somewhat exhausted, asked and was granted 3 sips of the mead. Some sips! He sucked up the mead in 3 swallows and, before the eyes of the horrified Gunlad, turned himself into an eagle and flew up, up, and away through a window high above in the cellar vault, carrying the exalting mead with him in his stomach.

By the ancient law of Wales, three things in the court were ordered to be told the king before being made known to any other person: every sentence of the judge, every new song, and every new cask of mead.

The Romans introduced grape growing to the British Isles. The Isle of Ely became so celebrated for the fruitfulness of its vintage that it was called the Isle of Vines.

William of Malmesbury wrote that Gloucester had "richer vineyards than any other county, the wine by no means ungrateful to the palate with no disagreeable sharpness of taste, being little inferior to the sweet wines of France."

Geoffrey of Monmouth averred, "Without the city walls of London the old Roman vines still put forth their green leaves and clusters in the plains of East Smithfield, in the fields of St. Gile's, and on the site where now stands Hatton Garden."

At the coronation of Richard II in the 14th century, wine of all kinds spouted from all the fountains and conduits, to the delight of medieval Londoners.

Of the 12th and 13th centuries, Holinshed said that "the strongest wines were in greatest request, and claret and other weak wines were little valued."

In the 14th century, French wine was such a glut on the market that it sold for 13 shillings and 4 pence per tun—less than a penny per gallon. French wines were inexpensive until the 19th century, the beginning of the age of the great and rich connoisseurs.

An English tavern sign of 1736 was inscribed, "Drunk for a penny, dead drunk for two pence, clean straw for nothing."

Circumstances being what they were, Englishmen of the 18th century got frightfully soused. To say of a man "He is an honest drunken fellow" was a compliment. "Jack," said a gentleman of very high quality when William was voted by Parliament into the vacant throne (1689), "Jack, go home to your lady, and tell her we have got a Protestant King and Queen, and go make a bonfire as big as a house, and bid the butler make ye all drunk, ye sly dog."

King Edward was murdered at a feast held in honor of St. Augustine. This happened in Puckle Church, Gloucestershire, A.D. 946. The king and all his nobles were so thoroughly plastered from the mulled wine they had drunk that they were unable to offer the slightest resistance to the intrepid regicide.

Richard III had his brother Clarence drowned in a butt of malmsy, his favorite drink—a nice brotherly touch.

Corks were not used until 1610, during the reign of King James I. Before that time bottles were stoppered up with rags or wicks steeped in tallow or beeswax.

Chambertin was Napoleon's favorite wine (but it was a bottle of cognac that consoled the emperor on his retreat from Moscow).

Edward VII, one of history's great connoisseurs, preferred Château Margaux. This so impressed Richard Milhous Nixon that, whenever sailing down the Potomac on the presidential yacht, he ordered the steward to fill his glass with $40-a-bottle Margaux, while serving his guests $6-a-bottle Châteauneuf-du-Pape. Nixon thought his guests wouldn't know the difference.

When it came to white wine, King Edward was partial to Château d'Yquem. He had this in common with Diamond Jim Brady.

French wines were already so superior in antiquity that the emperor Domitian ordered half of the vineyards of Gaul destroyed to give Italian wine makers a chance.

The Plantagenet kings of England and their well-to-do subjects were so fond of Bordeaux wines that a fleet of 300 vessels hardly sufficed to supply the English with French wines. Some say that the Hundred Years' War was fought partially to protect the innumerable vineyards in Aquitaine from being taken over by the French.

St. Joan of Arc liked to pour wine into her soup.

The name of the excellent and famous Rhône wine Châteauneuf-du-Pape ("ninth house of the pope") refers to the period of the "Babylonian captivity" (1309–1378), when many popes were French and lived at Avignon.

After the failure of the great Nivelles offensive of World War I, the French soldiers' daily ration of *pinard* (ordinary red wine) was increased from a half liter to a full liter.

Confronting the convenient cork

In 1397 King Wenceslaus of Bohemia paid a visit to King Charles VI of France to conclude an alliance. Wenceslaus was so enraptured by the good wines of Champagne that he said, "To hell with the treaty!" and stayed at Rheims for weeks and weeks guzzling. As Wenceslaus was an alcoholic and Charles stark mad, the treaty did not matter anyhow. (Wenceslaus is known mainly for once having spitted and roasted alive his cook for spoiling his meat and putting too much honey in his mead. "May you be cook and wine maker to King Wenceslaus!" was the worst curse in Bohemia at that time.)

The medieval French poet François Villon's favorite hangout was a Parisian tavern called Pet du Diable ("Devil's Fart"). It was very famous and very disreputable.

Oscar Wilde used to drown his sorrows at the Parisian Café Weber.

Toulouse-Lautrec would sometimes mingle together all the dregs left in bottles in a special cocktail of his own. He called the horrifying potion *Tremblement*—"the trembles."

Napoleon ordered 8 bottles of Château Lafite to be sent to Elba to console him during his exile on that island.

Bernkasteler is the name of a very old and well-known German wine. Centuries ago the count of Bernkastel was told by the village priest that the bishop of Trier was on his sickbed and that nothing could cure him. "Sayest thou so!" cried the count and at once visited the ailing prelate, carrying a small keg of his best wine on his shoulder. The bishop drank, and drank a little more, and drank until the wine was gone, got up with renewed vigor, and lived for many years in a happy daze, drinking Bernkasteler. The particular variety of this wine was from then on known as *Doktor*, it is said, because the good prelate exclaimed, "This is better than a physician!"

Historians pooh-pooh the tale of the good bishop of Trier. Bernkasteler Doktor, they say, derives its name from the Witwe Frau Doktor Hugo Thanisch, who happened to own the vineyard.

Villon's favorite Parisian dive

During the Thirty Years' War the Bavarian general Tilly besieged the town of Rothenburg ob der Tauber. After Rothenburg surrendered, Tilly, enraged at the city's stubborn resistance, ordered all the inhabitants killed. The burgomaster, a mighty winebibber before the Lord, knew Tilly to also have a vast capacity. He made the general a sporting proposition. "Let us have a drinking match," he said. "If your highness wins, you can chop our heads off, but if I should be the victor, you will spare the good burghers' lives." Tilly

was intrigued. The town had an official *Willkommen Humpen,* a huge beaker holding about 2 gallons. The thing to do was empty it all at one swallow. The general as well as the burgomaster managed to accomplish this task, but having done so, the general fell from his horse, while the burgomaster somehow remained standing upright and was declared the winner. The citizens were saved. Since then, every year on the anniversary of this remarkable bout, the mayor of Rothenburg has to reenact the wondrous event and empty the welcome *Humpen.* But he is cheating. Fastened to the inside rim of the beaker is a quite ordinary small glass of Rhine wine.

Of Moselle wine it was said, "It may be employed, under medical advice, to increase the appetite and stimulate the kidneys without heating the blood or brain."

The German town of Bacharach derives its name from Bacchus, the god of wine, who was worshipped there when the Rhine country was part of a Roman province. No wonder. Bacharach is situated smack in the center of the best wine-growing area in Germany. Nearby, on a rock overlooking the river, sat beautiful, lightly clad (an understatement) Lorelei, combing her long, strawberry blond hair, luring besotted boatmen to their doom in the waters of the Rhine below. Possibly the boatmen had drunk too much *Hock* (Hochheimer).

Rhine wine was supposed to "refresh the vapid tongue, enliven a tired nervous system, and open all the pores."

The most noble, and unattainable, wine of all, if you believe some Hungarians, was Imperial Tokay. An incredible amount of shriveled grapes were needed to make a decent amount of it. Whatever Imperial Tokay was made—and it was made only in exceptionally good years—belonged automatically to the court. Every bottle was numbered. His Apostolic Majesty, the Austrian emperor, gave away a bottle now and then to those he thought deserved it. At one time Catherine the Great of Russia had a few bottles of Imperial. A special detachment of cossacks was appointed to guard them. There is still Tokay Szamorodni, and the sweet Tokay Aszú, but they are not the old Imperial, which is now only a memory.

Lacryma Christi is a well-known wine from the Naples area. The name means "Tears of Christ," and it is said that the wine is so good because its vineyards, on the slopes of Mt. Vesuvius, were watered by Christ's tears. It is not clear why Christ cried. One explanation is that the beauty of the Bay of Naples moved him to tears; another is that he wept when he saw the terrible sins committed in the city.

An old Italian proverb says, "The bread of Padua, the tripe of Treviso, the whores of Venice, and the wine of Vicenza are the best of their kind in the world."

The Umbrian town of Orvieto was already famous for its lovely white wine during the Renaissance. While at work there on his "Last Judgment," Pinturicchio requested that part of his payment be made in the local wine.

The history of the name of the popular Italian white wine Est! Est!! Est!!! is particularly interesting. In the year 1111, Bishop Johann Fugger and his trusty manservant, Martin, were traveling to Rome to witness the coronation of Emperor Henry V by the pope. As they went along, the bishop, an ardent lover of fine wine, sent Martin ahead to sample the wines in the towns through which they were going to pass. Martin's instructions were to chalk the word *Est* ("it is") on the walls of those inns where the wine met with the bishop's standards.

At the town of Montefiascone, north of Rome, Martin found the local white wine so good that he exuberantly chalked up *Est! Est!! Est!!!* on the wall of the inn. Fugger agreed with his servant's estimation of Montefiascone's wine and, in fact, drank himself to death in the town (how long this took is a matter of conjecture). The good bishop is buried in Montefiascone, and the wine, thanks in large part to the tale of Johann and Martin, still enjoys great popularity.

It was Dom Pérignon, a Benedictine monk, who put the bubbly into champagne by accidentally getting some carbonic acid gas into his wine mixture. When he tried it for the first time, he exclaimed, "*Je bois des étoiles!*"—"I am drinking stars!" In honor of his great feat of fizzing, a statue of the good brother now stands in one of the city squares of Rheims.

Champagne at first ran into a great deal of resistance because Louis XIV's physician declared it would turn the king's blood into vinegar. When people were observed drinking it without their blood turning pale and sour, the new beverage began its triumphant rise until, nowadays, more than 100 million bottles are produced every year in France alone.

Enjoying some extra-dry sparkling wine

Thomas Jefferson, who grew very fond of it, said champagne keeps well, bears transportation with equanimity, and should not be drunk until it is 4 years old.

Otto von Bismarck, the "Iron Chancellor," was once invited to dinner by the kaiser. The emperor served Sekt, that is, German champagne, instead of the usual Moët et Chandon. "Your Majesty will excuse me," said Bismarck, "but I cannot bear German Sekt." "But for patriotism's sake," insisted William. "My patriotism does not extend to my stomach," said Bismarck, and was sacked by the All-Highest a short while later. Thus began the downfall of imperial Germany.

THERE GROWS NO VINE AS GROWS BY THE BEAUTIFUL RIVER: Wine in the Americas

Pressing California grapes

Wine has a long history in the New World. Before white men and wine there was *pulque,* a drink made from the maguey or agave plant, which was greatly loved by the Aztecs, who drank immense quantities of it. One has to swallow a lot of pulque to get tipsy, because its alcoholic content is low.

Maguey juice can also be distilled to make mescal and tequila—very strong drinks indeed. A white, fat worm floats in all mescal bottles. Without it the stuff would not be *original Mescal con su proprio gusano* ("the real thing with its worm").

Pulque was thought to be an invention of the lady Xochitl ("Flower"), who lived in the days of the 8th Toltec emperor.

Mayauel was the goddess of the maguey plant. She had 400 sons, who were all in some way concerned with pulque drinking. The stages of drunkenness were computed using the number of sons—or the number of their totem, the rabbit. Thus 10 rabbits stood for mild elation, 20 for cheerful tipsiness, and 400 rabbits meant being completely stoned. The chief pulque god was called Two Rabbits.

In the 10th century, Leif, a bold Viking and son of Eric the Red, made a landfall on the northeast coast of America. Among the crew of his longship was a German named Tyrker. Tyrker went exploring in the forest and came back with a load of wild grapes. Leif promptly named the new-found land *Vinland* ("Wine Land").

As soon as the French landed in Florida, they started making wine from wild grapes. Their settlement lasted only from 1562 to 1565. Then all the poor Frenchmen were massacred by the Spaniards, who wanted no competitors in that part of the world. Thus no wine was drunk for a while in North America.

Excavations disclosed that the Jamestown settlers had ice-storage pits for keeping their wine cool as early as 1608.

The first English governor of New York, Richard Nicholls, gave a patent to plant vines on Long Island near Southampton to a certain Paulus Richards. The governor was so enthusiastic about progress

The vine still flourishes on Long Island.

made that he voiced the opinion that New York wine could supply the wants of "all the Dominions of the Crown."

Wine grapes were grown on Manhattan until the middle of the 19th century.

That grapes grew wild in America is proven by such names as Martha's Vineyard. But Martha was really a Martin, a friend of Bartholomew Gosnold, the island's discoverer and namegiver.

Wine came to the American Southwest as early as 1630. Franciscan friars planted the first vineyard near the present town of Socorro, New Mexico. A hundred years later, Fray Francisco Dominguez found the Indians of Isleta Pueblo busy making wine from their own fine grapes.

In 1776 the 700 inhabitants of Albuquerque, according to one chronicler, "all had their little orchards with vinestocks."

The chieftain Arpad brought his Magyar tribes to settle in the plains of Hungary. The Magyar horsemen "cooked" their meat by keeping it under their saddles (hence "steak tartar"), and the only alcoholic beverage they had was fermented mares' milk. Arpad Haraszthy, a Hungarian nobleman who came to the valleys of California in 1849, brought wine making in the grand manner to the West Coast. Seeing the potentialities there, he had the state of California send him to Europe to bring back the choicest grapes. He returned with 200,000 cuttings, and got busy. The great wine industry of California was born. (The state never reimbursed Haraszthy for the expenses of the trip, which amounted to $12,000. Colonel Sutter, the owner of Sutter's Mill, said, "I told you so.")

Ambrose Bierce wrote that "the wine of Arpad Haraszthy has a bouquet all its own. It tickles and titillates the palate. It gurgles as it slips down the alimentary canal. It warms the cockles of the heart, and it burns the sensitive lining of the stomach."

The famous Catawba grapevine, one of 88 native vines identified in 1830 by an industrious botanist, was discovered by a certain John Adlum in 1802 in Buncombe County.

Of Catawba wine grapes grown on the shores of the Ohio River, the "Rhine of America," Longfellow sang:

There grows no vine
By the haunted Rhine,
By Danube or Guadalquivir,
Nor an island or cape,
That bears such a grape
As grows by the Beautiful River.

Thomas Jefferson once wrote that, "No nation is drunken where wine is cheap, and none sober, where the dearness of wine substitutes ardent spirits as the common beverage."

A DAMN'D SMALL BOTTLE: Port, Sherry, and Madeira

The Iron Duke meets a rat.

Port, sherry, and Madeira are "fortified wines"—they have been made stronger by the addition of alcohol.

Port originally came from Oporto in Portugal and was for centuries the rage in English clubs and regimental messes. Portuguese growers complained that Britons wanted port to feel like erupting Vesuvius in their stomachs, to burn like flaming gunpowder, and to look as black as ink. This was not exactly what the Portuguese thought port should be.

A typical military mess

When drunk in its native Portugal, port was originally not fortified very much. It was the English who insisted on having more and more brandy added to their favorite tipple, and the English were the main customers.

Port first appeared in England in 1689 and quickly became the favorite drink of the upper class.

The Duke of Wellington insisted on his daily generous measure of port. The Iron Duke liked to tell the story of how he had once found a rat in his bottle of port. Young Fitzroy Somerset ventured the opinion that it must have been a very small rat. "Damme," insisted His Grace, "it was a damn'd big rat!" Somerset thought then that the bottle must have been rather large. "Damme, Sir, it was a damn'd small bottle!" roared the duke. The dimensions of a fair-to-middling rat being well known, what did the Iron Duke consider a "damn'd small bottle" of port?

Sherry was the early English rendition of Jerez or Xerez de la Frontera, the chief city in the region of Spain that exports this particular fortified favorite.

Sherry was also known as "sherris," "sack," and "sac."

King Henry VIII once sent the saintly Sir Thomas More as ambassador to the Holy Roman emperor. In order to steady his nerves before meeting the mighty Hapsburg, Sir Thomas ordered his valet to bring him a large bumper of sack. He threw it down, ordered another, knocked that one back, called for a third, and finished that off in a similarly speedy fashion. He then asked for a fourth, but the servant, concerned that his master might not bring off his audience with the emperor in fitting form, dissuaded him (not without a lot of persuasion, however, going even so far as to hide the remaining sack). When Sir Thomas returned, he was livid with rage, threatening his valet with a cane: "You rogue, you low cur," he roared, "see what you have done to me! I spoke so eloquently to the emperor on the strength of those three bumpers of sack I drunk that he told me I was well fitted to govern three parts of the world. Now, you dog, if I had but drunk the fourth glass, I had been fit to govern all the world!"

Madeira comes from a small island off the coast of Africa, which, although only some 30 miles in length, is called the "Pearl of the Atlantic." Madeira's claim to fame rests upon three facts. First, it is good. Second, it was George Washington's favorite drink, and his contemporaries took their cue from him. Third, it lasts, and lasts, and lasts. The contents of an opened bottle of Madeira are still palatable 6 months later.

"If I had but drunk the fourth glass!"

In America, between 1765 and 1810, Madeira held the place of honor on every gentleman's table.

In 1789, on her way to join her husband in New York, Martha Washington paused at Philadelphia to give a party. The guests managed to imbibe the following: "10 bottles of Madeira, 1 bottle of Champagne, 2 bottles of claret, 45 bowls of punch, 10 bottles of American porter, 1 bottle of Taunton Ale, 2 bottles of crab cider." It was quite a shindig, and, of course, Madeira headed the list.

John Adams, who, as he himself wrote, was "fired with a zeal against ardent spirits, the multiplication of taverns, retailers and dram-shops and tippling-houses," yet recorded in his diary, when he was sitting in the Continental Congress at Philadelphia in 1774: "A mighty feast again. Nothing less than the best of Claret, Madeira, and Burgundy. I drank Madeira at a great rate and found no inconvenience."

Chief Justice John Marshall was brought up on "Madeira and Federalism"; the very best sort of Madeira was known as "Supreme Court."

Chief Justice John Marshall developed a rule, in the interest of moderation, that members of the Supreme Court should imbibe only on rainy days. Later, he and his eminent brothers regretted this resolution. They therefore amended their rule so that, whereas the Court held sway over the whole country, and whereas it was a reasonable assumption that some precipitation was always falling somewhere within the borders of the nation, every day was a rainy day on which the justices were permitted to sample the Court's wet goods.

Samuel Stearns, a friend of George Washington, wrote about the habits of the Father of Our Country: "He is very regular, temperate, and industrious. . . . At three he dines . . . and drinks half a pint to a pint of Madeira wine. This with one small glass of punch, a draught of beer, and two dishes of tea." Temperate!

THE GOOD CREATURE OF GOD: The history of hard liquor

An early alchemist in search of the Magic Elixir

In the old days, alcoholic beverages, especially hard liquor, were called "God's Good Creature," a gift from the compassionate deity to thirsty mankind.

The difference between hard liquor—also known as "hot waters" and "ardent spirits"—and small drink (wine, beer, and such) is that the latter are fermented, while the hard stuff is distilled.

In China, spirits were distilled from rice wine 2,000 years ago.

Pliny the Elder wrote, "Oh, wondrous craft! In some way or other it has been discovered that water might be made to render men drunk!"

The first actual mention of alcohol occurs in a history of the Saracens. The word *alcohol,* in fact, is Arabic, being a derivation of two words, *al* ("the") and *kohl,* a term for spirits distilled from wine. As pious Moslems, the Saracens distilled not in order to produce hot waters, but to find the elixir of life.

The word *distillation,* as also the word *still* (as in "pot still"), derives from the Latin *distillare,* meaning "dripping downward."

The word *spirit* originally meant "breath" or "wind motion," and in the course of time it came to denote spirituous liquors, which invigorate like breath or fresh air.

The first distilleries were set up at Sabur and Damascus in Syria about A.D. 900.

The earliest distillers were all alchemists. The word *alchemist* is derived from the Arab *al* ("the") and *kimya* ("chemistry"), which in turn came from the Greek *chemeia* and *chumeia* ("a mingling").

While the alchemists were trying to create the "Universal Medicine" and the "Magic Elixir" and, especially, to transmute base metals into gold, by the fortunate workings of serendipity they stumbled upon spirits of great strength. One saintly Arab alchemist, when surrounded by enemies, jumped into and dissolved himself in his own *aqua fortis*—that is, "strong water."

Albertus Magnus, born in 1206, was the first great European alchemist. He is said to have been excessively stupid as a boy. He also discovered and tasted—as a scientific experiment—strong distilled waters, and was accused of having been inspired to it by the devil.

The Catalonian Arnold de Villanova, in his works *Thesaurus Thesaurorum* and *Rosarium Philosophorum*, was the first to write a treatise on how to obtain alcohol by the distillation of wine. He was convinced that he had discovered the elixir of life. Pope Clement V heard about this and named Arnold his personal physician and sampled the elixir. After Arnold de Villanova's death in 1310, his works were burned as heretical by order of the church.

The Spaniard Raymond Lully, a student of Arabic alchemy, wrote a work, *Opera Alchima*, in which he described making the "True Water of Life." He called the product of his labors *aqua vitae* ("water of life"), from which derive *aquavit*, *usquebaugh*, *whiskey*, and *eau de vie*.

Distillation for the purpose of making ardent spirits commercially began in France in the early 1400s. In 1514 a guild was formed in Paris that lumped together the makers of sauces, vinegar, lemonade, and eau de vie. The Good Creature was finally on its way to the stomachs of the masses.

In his *Chronicles* (1577), Holinshed spoke favorably about aqua vitae: "It sloweth age, it strengtheneth youth, it helpes digestion, it cutteth phlegm, it abandoneth melancholy, it relisheth the heart, it cureth hydropsia, it healeth the strangurie, it pounceth the stone, it expelleth gravel, it puffeth away ventositie, it keepeth the head from whirling, the eyes from dazzling, the tongue from lisping, the mouth from snaffling, the teeth from chattering, and the throat from rattling; it keepeth the weasand from stiffling, the stomach from wambling, and the heart from swelling—it keepeth the hands from shivering, the sinews from shrinking, the bones from aching, and the marrow from soaking."

Ardent spirits can be made of practically everything found on this earth. Brandy comes from grape wine, slivovitz from plums, vodka from potatoes, aquavit from sawdust, barack palinka from apricots, kirsch from cherries, kümmel from caraway seeds and anisette, absinthe from wormwood, Calvados and applejack from apples, gin from molasses, bourbon from corn, whiskey from rye, mescal and tequila from agave cactus, arrack from palm sap and dates. Hard stuff can be produced from rice, beets, sugar, string, old leather, and hairy caterpillars.

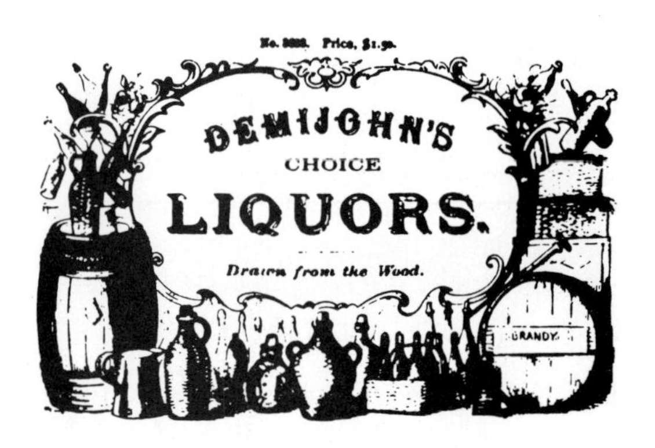

Possibly the vilest (from a Western point of view) liquor was *yan-yang-tskew*, a Chinese rotgut made from fermented sheep's flesh and, in one province, from the fermenting carcasses of plump puppy dogs. "Lamb-wine" was said to be especially strong, a favorite among Tartars and Mongols. Genghis Khan liked it.

The 19th-century author Ralph Grindrod wrote: "It is known that the Swedes, whose propensity for strong drink is well known, flavor their brandy by distilling over with it a large species of the black ant. These insects contain a resin, an oil, and an acid, which are highly valued for the flavour and potency which they impart to the brandy. They are found in abundance at the bottom of fir-trees, in small, round hills, and are taken in that state for use."

Macerated wormwood is one of the main ingredients of absinthe, a highly toxic liquor running between 70 percent and 80 percent alcohol. Absinthe has the characteristic aromatic flavor of wormwood, known as *Artemisia absinthium*, blended with little items like angelica root, sweet flag, dittany leaves, star anise, hyssop, and fennel. In other words, it is a strange herb-alcohol brew acting potently on the nerve ganglia. Too much can cause hallucinations—what we have come to call DTs.

Absinthe was first drunk by French soldiers engaged in the conquest of Algeria during the 1830s. French army doctors advised the men to pour a good dash of absinthe into their exceedingly bad drinking water in order to "kill the Cholera microbes." Absinthe sure enough poisoned the bacilli, but it also poisoned the troopers, who were, however, a hardy lot and "iron-throated." They liked the flavor and, from about 1850 on, absinthe became the favorite French before-noon drink.

Absinthe was poisonously green, and the time of day when it was sipped was called *l'Heure Verte*—"the green hour."

Absinthe played a great part in the folklore of Paris. Verlaine, Arthur Symons, and Toulouse-Lautrec are said to have killed themselves with it. On the other hand, Henri Rousseau, Le Douanier, Guillaume Apollinaire, Guy de Maupassant, and others drank absinthe daily without suffering bad effects. (Syphilis did Maupassant in, not booze.) But all these anise fanciers drank absinthe very moderately and in a proportion of one part wormwood to nine parts of other things.

According to the American humorist George Ade, "Absinthe drinks were the most powerful pick-me-ups that lifted the sufferer about a mile in the air and then let him drop in the mud."

Absinthe reached the height of fashion in the Paris of the 1890s. Famous artists used the places where it was drunk as motifs for their paintings. *The Absinthe Drinkers*, by Degas, shows some very far-gone customers with a smashed-out-of-their-skulls, vacant, and staring look in their eyes.

Absinthe was first made commercially in Switzerland, not France. Famous French aperitifs other than absinthe include Byrrh, Amer Picon, and Pernod.

The deleterious effects of absinthe were perceived in the early 1900s. When absinthe was outlawed in the French army and navy in 1912, the Foreign Legionnaires rioted in the taverns of Sidi-Bel-Abbes. In 1914 the serving of absinthe was outlawed in France "as a war measure," and outlawed it remained. In the United States absinthe was prohibited in 1917. It was supposed to cause an illness called "absinthism, characterized by vertigo, accompanied by an unconscious state of automatism in which criminal actions are accomplished."

Many French whodunits were based on crimes committed unwittingly by otherwise respectable men while under the influence of too much absinthe.

Vermouth comes from the German word for wormwood—*Wermuth.* It was also known as the "green devil." While absinthe was made from the leaves of the wormwood, vermouth gets a small infusion of the yellow flowers of the plant, much milder in their effect, but very flavorful, giving vermouth its characteristic taste. The main ingredient of vermouth is wine, red or white as the case may be, so it is not an ardent spirit.

Vermouth was known as "wormwood wine" in the days of Shakespeare.

Aquavit is the Scandinavian's hard drink. It is distilled from potatoes and barley and was first manufactured in Aalborg, Denmark, some 150 years ago.

A certain Professor Huss described the moderate Swedish aquavit drinker in 19th-century Stockholm: "Rising early in the morning, according to the season, he takes a cup of coffee mixed with a glass of aquavit. He then attends to his occupation until nine o'clock, when he takes breakfast and a second glass of aquavit. At his dinner, at noon, he has another glass or two. At five or six, he again has a glass; and lastly, with his supper, at eight or nine, still another. He thus consumes six large glasses regularly every day, enjoying all the time a character among his friends as a person of great moderation, who scarcely takes what is requisite for an individual in his station."

When the Carthusian monks left France for the more hospitable (to them) Spain, Father Rey, their abbot, absolutely balked at giving the French government, which had bought the order's buildings and land at auction, the secret of their famous Chartreuse liqueur. The Carthusians still make it in four varieties: the Elixir, the Yellow, the Green, and the White. Now only Yellow and Green, 86 and 110 proof, are commercially available.

The formula for Chartreuse was given to the good fathers in 1605 to brew in their mountain retreat at Grenoble by le Maréchal d'Estrées in gratitude for prayers that the monks performed for him during a severe illness.

Benedictine was first made by the Benedictine monks in 1510 at their monastery at Fécamp on the wind-swept Channel coast. It became popular among the nobility after jolly, long-nosed, and amorous Roi François I declared it his favorite potation.

The composition of Benedictine remains a trade secret, but it is thought to contain fresh lemon peel, cardamons, hyssop, angelica, peppermint, thyme, cinnamon, nutmeg, cloves, and arnica, mixed and macerated.

Even though it is no longer made by the monks, Benedictine bottles still prominently display the letters D.O.M., standing for *Deo Optimo Maximo* ("God most good, most great"). Benedictine is also sold mixed with brandy under the name B & B.

Vodka is Russian for "little water."

The Russian army when in the field carries a portable distillery with every battalion to assure a constant supply of vodka, which is made from potatoes.

One of vodka's greatest attractions has always been that it leaves no odor of alcohol on the drinker's breath. During the 1950s, one brand was advertised under the slogan "Wifey won't know."

The Poles are the greatest per-capita consumers of hard liquor—1.5 gallons yearly. Most of that is vodka.

Gin was first made by a Dutch chemist, Mynheer Sylvius van Leyden. He gave his liquid refreshment the name of *genièvre,* meaning "juniper" in French, because juniper berries were used as one of the main ingredients. The name was rendered into Dutch to read "geneva," out of which the English made "gin." Others say that gin derived its name from the first syllables of the Italian or Spanish *ginebra,* meaning the like-named city in Switzerland, which has absolutely nothing to do with gin. During Prohibition, some Americans thought that *gin* came from hydro*gen*—"gin and water." Since good Professor Sylvius set up his first distillery in Schiedam, gin was also known as "Schiedam schnapps" or "Holland waters." By whatever name it went, it hit the British Isles like an earthquake, turning them into an "Ocean of Gin."

At first, gin was sold in apothecaries as a precious panacea for all kinds of illnesses and, especially, as a diuretic.

As in the case of the telephone, the propeller, the automobile, and the airplane, many besides Mynheer Sylvius claimed to be the creators of geneva. The French say that it was one of good King Henri IV's sons, M. le Comte de Morret, who first flavored wine spirits with juniper berries. Though juniper wine in his native Navarre was called *le vin des pauvres,* "the wine of the poor," the count declared that he was not ashamed to be seen drinking it, but that he owed exuberant health and a sexually active ripe old age to his own creation, *le vin genièvre.*

It was good Protestant William of Orange, who, following the Glorious Revolution of 1689, brought gin to London from his native Holland. It so happened that William was almost continuously at war with Louis XIV of France. He therefore tried to cut off imports of French wine and put prohibitive taxes on them. Soon only the wealthy could afford what little French wines were available. Gin, on the other hand, was ridiculously cheap. One could get drunk on a penny, and stinking drunk on 1½ pence. Gin became the tipple of the poor.

Between 1740 and 1750, at the height of the "Gin Epoch," deaths in London outnumbered births by two to one, "because of bad gin," it was said. There were both "Holland gin" and "London gin." Holland gin was supposed to be taken straight. Taking London gin neat was inviting disaster.

Gin drinking was encouraged by the landed gentry, who controlled Parliament and made laws concerning spirituous liquors. Defoe said more grain was used making gin than making bread, and grain destined to become tipple brought more than that slated to become food. The gentry liked that. They themselves never drank the stuff.

Gin and other "burning waters" were sold in the streets by so-called brandy women.

Gin was given to English workmen as part of their wages during the 18th century.

London gin was made of wine spirits, juniper berries, cardamon, angelica root, sulphuric acid, oil of turpentine, sugar, coriander, and cassia. One ounce of juniper oil will flavor 100 gallons of modern gin.

A bad sort of gin consumed in colonial America was called Strip and Go Naked.

In the United States, beer, rye, and bourbon were the drinks of the corner saloon's customers. Gin was frowned upon by Americans before Prohibition, and men felt self-conscious ordering it before company. On the other hand, before 1920 it was generally believed to be a cure for all urinary troubles. A man caught ordering gin would sheepishly explain, "It's for me kidneys," or say with an awkward smile, "I drink it for the wife's kidneys."

THAT HOT, HELLISH, AND TERRIBLE LIQUOR: Rum

A political use of rum

Neither the Puritans nor the Founding Fathers took to gin. What they liked was rum, straight or in a number of mixtures. Rum is the original American strong drink, the hot waters from the New World. Even its name is American.

An ancient manuscript describing the West Indian island of Barbados shortly after it was settled by the English in 1651 says, "The chief fudling they make is Rumbullion, alias Kill-Divil, and this is made of sugar canes distilled, a hot, hellish, and terrible liquor."

There was "rumbullion," "rumscullion," "rumbooze," "rumbowling," and "rumfustian," all originally the same "hellish liquor." Rumbowling eventually became the name for rum-based sailors' grog. Rumbooze or rambooze became a favorite of Oxford dons, made of eggs, ale, rum, and sugar. Gypsies were supposed to have invented it. Rumfustian was made of a quart of strong beer, a bottle of sherry, half a pint of gin, half a pint of rum, 12 egg yolks, orange peel, nutmeg, spices, and sugar. (The word *fustian* originally meant "substitute" or "fake," which would indicate that rumfustian was at first a pretended rum drink with no rum in it.) There was also "rumbarge," a drink that contained no rum at all.

New Englanders quickly shortened "rumbullion" to plain "rum." The first American reference to it, by its shortened name, is in a Massachusetts ordinance from 1657 prohibiting the sale of burning waters, "whether known by the name of rumme, strong water, wine, brandy, etc., etc."

The syllable *rum* is said to derive from either *aroma* or *saccharum*, the Latin word for sugar.

Rum was indeed made from sugar, distilled in the West Indies as early as 1550. It was a favorite among Sir Henry Morgan's buccaneers. Before it was discovered that sugar could be made from beets, the only source of the sweet stuff was sugar cane, and all the cane in the known world was in the Caribbean islands. Rum was first distilled in Barbados, then in Jamaica, where it became the chief article of export, and later in St. Croix, Cuba, and Puerto Rico.

Rum was also known as "Barbados-water," "Barbados-brandy," or "Jamaica-liquor" after the place where it was made. For a long time it was simply called Kill-Devil, not as a colloquial expression, but as an established trade name. The Dutch called it "brandywine," though it had neither brandy nor wine in it.

The Caribbean islands that produced sugar cane, that is molasses, that is rum, were so incredibly rich that, after the Seven Years' War, the British offered the French all of Canada in exchange for the small island of Guadaloupe. The French refused the offer.

It is said that the English eventually managed to inveigle the Indians to be allied with them instead of with the French, because they could produce rum in larger quantities and more cheaply than the French could supply brandy.

Dartmouth College, originally founded to educate Indian students to become "civilized Christians," was established with rum money.

Eleazar Wheelock was a very pious man;
He went into the wilderness to teach the In-di-an,
With a Gradus ad Parnassum, a bible, and a drum,
And five hundred gallons of New England Rum.
Eleazar was the faculty; and the whole curriculum
Was five hundred gallons of New England Rum!

The learned Reverend Increase Mather complained: "It is an unhappy thing that in later years a Kind of Drink called Rum has been common among us. They that are poor and wicked, too, can for a penny make themselves drunk." Being poor, of course, was a sign of God's displeasure. The wages of wickedness were poverty and rum. The wages of holiness were wealth, claret, and Madeira.

Lord Byron wrote, "There's naught, no doubt, so much the spirit calms as rum and true religion."

In 1855 Walt Whitman could still write in New York of "the liquor-bar lean'd against by the young rum-drinker and the old rum-drinker."

An encounter in a grogshop

Grog was the sailor's cold weather drink, a mixture of half rum and half water, with sugar added, served piping hot. Grog was named after "Old Grog," Admiral Edward Vernon, who got his nickname from a coat he always wore, made of grogam, alternating wool and silk threads. Vernon gave his seamen a daily ration of grog to prevent scurvy. Lime juice would have been a lot better for the purpose, but could not hold a candle to rum, as far as the jolly tars were concerned.

The bloody pirate Bartholomew Roberts' much-feared Jolly Roger showed, on a red ground, Roberts and a skeleton toasting each other with a flagon of rum.

When cruel Captain William Bligh of the *Bounty* and his officers were cast adrift in an open boat and began their epic 3,618-mile voyage to Timor, it was rum that saved them. "The little rum we had," wrote the captain, "was a great service. When our nights were particularly distressing, I generally served a teaspoon or two to each person, and it was joyful tidings when they heard of my intentions."

Lord Horatio Nelson, after falling victim to a musket ball at the battle of Trafalgar, was preserved, literally, in a large keg of rum, which kept his body in prime condition for his lying in state in London. "No more felicitous death for a sailor" supposedly was the prince regent's comment.

Rum helped bring about the American Revolution. In 1733 England put high import duties and taxes on molasses, except that made in the home country and shipped in British ships. This threatened New England's economy and raised the price not only of the beloved rum, but also of the even more delectable punch and flip that were made with rum. Also, not enough rum was made in the colonies to quench the mighty colonial thirst, and, to top it all, English molasses was inferior! So all true "Sons of Libertie" drank damnation to the British Parliament, and, following John Hancock's example, took to smuggling rum in Yankee ships. Tempers flared until, at last, the embattled farmer stood his ground against ministerial tyranny.

As John Quincy Adams said, "I know not why we should blush to confess that molasses [for rum] was an essential ingredient in American independence."

Hot Buttered Rum was a favorite of George Washington, who often had a stirrup cup of it when passing a tavern—that is, he remained on his horse while the landlord brought the mug out to him, and he downed that "drink which warmed the cockles of his heart" in the saddle.

Calibogus or Bogus was unsweetened rum and ale taken cold. Some landlords put too little rum in their brew, hence *bogus* for "swindle."

Brandy was at first a strong rival to rum but eventually lost out to it. In 1682 one Thomas Ashe related that Carolina folks were making "by maceration, when duly fermented, a strong spirit, like brandy . . . with the help of an alembic."

Brandy comes from the German *Branntwein*—"burned wine." George Washington lost a battle at Brandywine, so named because the people in the vicinity both made and were addicted to the brew. Cheap brandy was also called *schnapps* by the Dutch and German settlers.

Brandy was first introduced to the world at the wedding of Henry II of France (then duke of Orléans) to Catherine de Medici. Henry III is said to have steadied his nerves with brandy during the massacres of St. Bartholomew's Day. But brandy was drunk 200 years before that by local connoisseurs in Armagnac country.

The noble brandy cognac can lawfully be called cognac only if it comes from Cognac. It has been said by some historians that Napoleon never touched Napoleon brandy, a most excellent potable. On the other hand, Joachim Murat, marshal of France and grand duke of Berg, downed a bottle of Armagnac at Eylau, then rallied his 70 squadrons of cavalry, drew his saber, and roared, "Follow my asshole!"—14,000 troopers did so. Armagnac has that kind of effect on a bold, high-strung man.

Brandy always helps end meals with a smile.

Armagnac is probably the oldest brandy. It was first distilled in 1411.

Punch was the favorite before-dinner drink of the Founding Fathers. It came from India. *Punch* is a Hindi word—*panch* or *punj*, meaning "five," from the 5 ingredients that went into the making of it: tea, arrack, sugar, lemons, and water. The "five" also stood for its 5 properties: hot, cold, sweet, bitter, and strong.

Colonial dames entertained their lady friends with punch made "genteel and palatable for a lady's delicate constitution" by addition of milk or cream.

Taverns and clubs had their own jealously guarded punch recipes, the most famous American one being Fish House Punch from Schuylkill, Pennsylvania, first quaffed in 1732 and "unimproved for 200 years for the simple reason that it could not be improved upon."

IT IS APT TO STOP YOUR POCKET WATCH:
Whiskey

The popularity of whiskey has little to do with how it's spelled.

Whiskey was the last of the major ardent spirits to arrive on the drinking scene. It eventually became "The American Drink," but only well after the Revolution.

Achille Murat, son of Joachim Murat, marshal of France and king of Naples, averred that whiskey was "the Best part of the American Government," a thing that could console a man for having to leave France.

The word *whiskey* is said to derive from *usquebaugh—uisque beatha,* the "water of life." *Uisge* is the Irish-Gaelic word for water. "Whiskey" is the common American spelling, while "whisky" is more frequently used in Scotland.

Aeneas McDonald asserts that the first civilized person to taste whiskey was the emperor Julian the Apostate, who, during his campaigns against barbaric tribes, was offered an alcoholic drink made from barley.

The Irish claim that St. Patrick brought whiskey to the Green Isle sometime around A.D. 400.

In Scotland whiskey was already drunk well before 1500, mostly in the castles of Scottish lairds who manufactured the stuff for their own use. It was said that they could down it in huge quantities without showing any effects.

One shining example of monstrous capacity was Martin Power, a farmer from Skye, who celebrated his 72nd birthday in 1837. For 50 years he drank, on an average, 30 glasses of whiskey per diem. On one occasion, he drank 23 pints of cider in less than an hour; on another, between four o'clock in the evening and dawn the following morning, together with four others, he downed 63 gallons of cider, plus 2 quarts of brandy. One day this remarkable man downed all by himself 4 quarts of raw whiskey, on another day a record 50 glasses of whiskey. At a calculation of 30 glasses per day for 50 years (rather an understatement), Power demolished no less than 37 hogsheads and 23 gallons of the hard stuff.

The Irish author Staynhurst wrote in 1577 on Irish whiskey: "Being moderately taken, it sloweth age, it strengtheneth youth, it helpeth digestion, it cutteth flegme, it abandoneth melancholie, it relisheth the heart, it quickeneth the mind, it lighteneth the spirit. And trulie it is a soveraigne liquor."

In Ireland whiskey is affectionately known as "the crathur" ("creature"), "juice of the barley," "hard tack," or "the foxy devil." The moonshine made in a copper pot still set in the turf-heated fireplace is called "poteen," which resembles the "poit du," the "black pot," of the Highlanders.

The Irish used whiskey to inspire death-defying ardor in much the same way that Middle Eastern assassins used hashish. The fierce knight Sir Savage, in 1350 before joining battle, had every man in his army given a generous triple swig of usquebaugh.

During the Elizabethan age, the great Shane O'Neill, before fighting the English, reputedly drank such a huge amount of the strongest usquebaugh that his men had to bury him up to his neck in cool, moist earth to counteract the heat and rage engendered by the fierce brew.

One commander, Christopher Ponese, carried the "encourage them with whiskey" stratagem too far. Besieged in Castle Maynooth, he gave his men so much usquebaugh that he made them sleepy instead of brave, and the English overcame the snoring defenders without trouble.

The Irish had Irish whiskey. The Scots had Scotch. Good Highland Scotch was effectively sealed off from the rest of the world until the battle of Culloden in 1746, when the Highland Jacobites were defeated by English Hanoverians. The redcoats then built roads to penetrate the north, down which Scotch whiskey began to flow, slowly at first, rapidly and in quantity later.

According to Hood's *Comick Almanack* of 1867, "On the event of a decease, everyone gets a glass [of ardent spirits] who comes within the door until the funeral, and for six weeks after it."

The oldest reference to Scotch is in a document of 1494 stating that Friar John Cor was given 8 bolls of malt to transform into aqua vitae.

The recipe for Drambuie, a wonderful whiskey liqueur, was given to Captain Mackinnon by Bonnie Prince Charlie after the disaster of Culloden, in gratitude for the captain having hidden him from the lobsterbacks on the island of Skye. Drambuie comes from *an dram buidheach*—meaning the "drink that satisfies." The recipe was guarded jealously by the Mackinnons for their own private use until 1906, when they began making Drambuie commercially.

Drambuie's Irish counterpart is Irish Mist, made at Tullamore since 1829. It is said to inspire the recitation of poetry, besides being a cure for the common cold.

George Washington made whiskey from rye, with a little Indian corn added.

It was the Scotch-Irish, steeped in whiskey lore and weaned on it, who after the Seven Years' War (the French and Indian War) and the Revolution swarmed into the western Pennsylvania wilderness, taking their pot stills with them. They planted corn, barley, potatoes, and, especially, rye.

The Whiskey Rebellion of 1794 was a serious affair. George Washington, himself a home brewer and distiller, felt that he had to uphold the law of the land (in this case an excise tax on whiskey that was hated in particular by the Scotch-Irish settlers in the Alleghenies). He assembled an army to crush the Monongahela Rye Uprising—no less than 15,000 men were mobilized, as many as had opposed the British lobsterbacks during the American Revolution.

Liquid Ecstasy was what connoisseurs called Conestoga rye, a brand of Monongahela rye made by the Gibson Distillery from 1840 on.

Old Monongahela, given to Irish laborers as part of their wages, is said to have "built Pennsylvania's early railroads, yard for yard."

The Kentucky humorist Irvin S. Cobb said that corn likker "tastes like the Wrath of God. It smells like gangrene rising in a mildewed silo. When you absorb a deep swig of it, you have all the sensations of having swallowed a lighted kerosene lamp. It will stop your pocket watch, snap your suspenders and crack your glass eye right across."

One Evans Williams was the first man to make corn likker in Kentucky, in 1783 at his Louisville distillery "on Fifth and Water Street."

Bourbon was also known as "red likker," the "liquid ruby," the "red creature," and "that famous soul-inspirin' liquah; the joy of every American father, the pride of every American mother, and for which American children cry."

Bourbon gets its color from being aged in charred wood barrels. Nobody had ever thought of coloring whiskey this way. It was purely an accident. According to legend a no-good, low-down, cheating barrel maker accidentally burned the insides of some of his kegs and sold this "inferior" product to a distiller without telling him about the problem. After having aged his whiskey in the charred kegs, the distiller, when broaching them, found that his liquor had turned a pleasant tangerine hue without in any way affecting the flavor. The man tried to sell the strange-looking brew and found to his delight that people liked the color. Red seemed nicer than no color (the natural state of whiskey).

Another explanation of the charred barrels used in making bourbon has it that a fish dealer purposely burned the insides of his old barrels to get rid of the awful, rotten fish stink. A bargain-hunting whiskey maker bought the barrels because they were so cheap, and then . . .

It is said by historians that it was the Reverend Elijah Craig who created bourbon. Craig was manufacturing and selling red likker aged in charred oak barrels in the year 1789.

Red likker eventually got the name bourbon because most of it was made in Bourbon County, Kentucky—most, but not all.

It was at Thomas Jefferson's suggestion that Bourbon County got its name, in honor of King Louis XVI, a Bourbon king of France and ally of America, whose regiments, under the command of General Rochambeau, helped Washington defeat Cornwallis at Yorktown.

Bourbon County no longer produces bourbon.

Bourbon is manufactured at a proof not exceeding 160—that is, 80 percent alcohol. ("Proof" is a measure of the strength of ardent spirits and is given as twice the percent of alcohol.)

The word *bourbon* first appeared on the label of a whiskey bottle in 1846.

It is said that in the famous Mint Julep the bourbon and mint are joined together in holy wedlock.

A certain Captain Marryat wrote in 1839: "They say that you may always know the grave of a Virginian as, from the quantity of juleps he has drunk, mint invariably springs up where he has been buried."

An Englishwoman, Mrs. Frances Trollope, was not overly impressed by American julep fanciers: "They drink mint julap (*sic*) and chew tobacco and spit, swearing by the Beard of Jupiter that they are very graceful and agreeable."

A certain George D. Prentice, tired of being frequently "called out" to defend his honor, devised a new kind of duel: a keg of bourbon would be placed between the seated antagonists, each of whom was armed with a straw. At the command "Fire!" the feuding gentlemen had to begin sucking with might and main. He who first fell insensible from his chair was declared "dead." For this novel mode of fighting a duel, Prentice was declared a "cad and coward" and was advised to leave Kentucky for good unless he wanted his body ventilated with bullets.

Buffalo Bill Cody loved his bourbon, and whenever anybody invited him to "have one on him," Cody's reply invariably was, "Sir, you are speaking the language of my tribe." But then someone convinced Bill that he was drinking too much for his own good, and the famous frontiersman and producer of the Wild West Show swore a solemn oath in front of witnesses that he would henceforth limit himself to a single glass of whiskey per diem. Unfortunately, being held to his vow made Cody melancholy, nervous, and irascible. But he did not want to go back on his word. A friend found the ideal solution to the problem by presenting Buffalo Bill with a glass snifter holding a quart of the red essence. Thus Cody could keep his word and enjoy his usual generous measure, shedding quickly all melancholy.

When Abraham Lincoln referred to Gen. Ulysses S. Grant as one of the most promising officers in the army, someone said, "Mr. President, Grant drinks." "Does he?" remarked Lincoln. "I wish I knew what whiskey he drinks. I would order some for the other generals in the army." Modern research has answered Honest Abe's question: Grant preferred Old Crow.

Both Andrew Jackson and Daniel Webster are said to have loved Old Crow.

As one contemporary recorded: "Old Jimmy Crow—Mysterious Jimmy they called him. He was an eccentric Scotchman who dropped in here about 1835 from nobody ever knew exactly where—because he wouldn't tell—and started the first, and for a long time the only, sizable commercial distillery that we had in Kentucky."

U. S. Grant and a bottle of his favorite whiskey

WHY THIS STRANGE NAME?
The story of the cocktail

Nathaniel Hawthorne mentions having downed a Tom and Jerry in New England during the 1830s.

It is said that a New York tavern wench and widow of a Revolutionary soldier concocted exhilarating mixed drinks for American officers and their French allies. One day these gentlemen raided a British headquarters and came back with a brace of male fowls, which they asked Betsy to roast for them. In honor of the occasion, the lusty barmaid decorated her bottles and tankards with rooster feathers and also used a feather to stir up her concoctions. On the spur of the moment the boisterous officers began calling "for one more cocktail." One Continental major rose and proposed a toast: "Here's to Betsy and her soul-inspiring drink. It tickles the palate with the same delightful sensations as the cock's tail feathers present to the eye!" They then drank there huzzahs to "the Cocktail!" Thus the name was born in the same year that saw the birth of the Constitution.

Others tell a different story. It was a Yankee clipper captain, engaged in the opium trade, who mixed one up for a Chinese mandarin of coral-button rank. "What is this wonderful drink called?" inquired the official. "It's a cocktail." "Why this strange name?" "Drink it, Your Excellency, and you will feel rooster feathers growing from your backside."

Some trace the origin of the cocktail back to antiquity, saying that the famous physician Claudius Galen invented it for the benefit of the emperor Commodus, "who may be allowed, without controversy, to have required pick-me-ups as often as any man alive." Galen's recipe called for a "cyathus of *spiritus vini gallici.*" *Cyathus* supposedly became *cocktail.*

There is also the tale of an Aztec maiden called Xochitl ("Flower"), who presented her own special kind of liquid refreshment to a delighted Montezuma. He smacked his lips and called the drink *xoctl,* after the fair damsel. Also, the refreshment was offered in an effigy jar in the shape of a *coyotl* ("coyote"). So, naturally, it is argued that *xoctl* and *coyotl* eventually became *cocktail.*

Kentuckians claim a different derivation for the word *cocktail.* Race horses had their tails "docked" so that they stuck up like rooster feathers. From that came a popular song of long ago, "Horsey Keep Your Tail Up!" This inspired southern racing fans to call their mixed drinks *cocktails.*

Other espousers of a Kentucky provenance for *cocktail* claim the word comes from cockfighting. Gentlemen assembled in taverns to describe the bellicose feats of their respective birds and told tall tales after the manner of fishermen. They quaffed mixed drinks, calling for "another cock tale." From there to *cocktail* was only a tiny step.

Englishmen maintain that Yorkshiremen called their fresh and foaming beer *cocktail.* The overflowing foam supposedly described a curve like a rooster's tail.

Frenchmen insist that *cocktail* is a Gallicism derived from *coquetel,* a famed burning sensation served in Bordeaux taverns by a certain Mademoiselle Octelle.

The town of Bladensburg, Maryland, claims to be the "Mother of the Cocktail." According to the good citizens of Bladensburg, the first cocktail was concocted by one John Welby Henderson, to revive a dueling gentleman named Hopkins. Hopkins was carried to Henderson's bar unconscious from the effects of a saber cut and the sight of blood gushing from his opponent's wounds. Henderson shook up a mixture of whiskey, syrup, and bitters that swiftly revived the duelist, who rose cockily with his "tail feathers up."

According to denizens of New York, Dutch *frouws* of New Amsterdam used brooms made of roosters' tails to sweep up their dining rooms. In the morning *mynheer* would pluck one of the feathers and use it to stir himself up an eye-opener mixed from Schiedam schnapps, sugar, and water.

The Squire's Recipes, published in 1748, has an item titled "A Cocktail": "By this curious name the Squire has designated a most delicious drink, the composition of which has long been held secret.

That it is of romantic origin the Squire admits, inasmuch as he secured the recipe straight from sweet Mistress Peggy Van Eyk, of the Inn called the Cock's Tail Tavern, at Yonkers." Peggy, according to the story, picked up a feather dropped by a rooster on her bar, and stirred up with it a drink for her loving swain, John Appleton, who promptly dubbed it *cocktail.*

The great Professor Jerry Thomas claimed to be the originator of the Martini, which he said he first served at San Francisco's Occidental Bar in 1860. It was first named Martinez, either after a gold miner or after a frostbitten man on his way to Martinez, California. The original recipe written down by Thomas himself in 1862 is:

1 dash of bitters
2 dashes of maraschino
1 jigger of gin
1 wine glass of vermouth
2 small lumps of ice

Shake thoroughly and strain into a large cocktail glass. Put ¼ slice lemon in the glass and serve.

Jeremiah Thomas (the "Professor") was born in 1825 at New Haven, Connecticut. Though his father had marked him out for the ministry, he became instead the foremost bartender of his age, untiring in his invention of drinks. He is best remembered for his two cold-weather creations, the Tom and Jerry and the Blue Blazer.

When Thomas was tending bar in San Francisco's famous El Dorado, a hirsute, unwashed miner, his pockets full of gold dust and a bowie knife stuck in his boot, emerged from the wilderness and, disdaining mere sissified whiskey, roared, "Booze-Boss, fix me up some hellfire that'll shake me down right to my gizzard!" Thomas rose to the challenge: "Come back in an hour, friend, I shall have something for you then." When the forty-niner returned, Thomas solemnly placed two large silver mugs on the bar. "Gentlemen," he announced in a sonorous voice, "you are about to witness the birth of a new beverage!" He poured a tumblerful of Scotch whiskey into one of the mugs, adding a slightly smaller quantity of boiling water, and with his "lucifer" ignited the liquid, which burst into a blue flame that rose to the ceiling. As the crowd shrunk back in awe, he hurled the blazing mixture back and forth between the two mugs, with a rapidity and a dexterity that were well-nigh unbelievable. This amazing spectacle continued in full movement for perhaps ten seconds, and then Professor Thomas quickly poured the beverage into a tumbler and smothered the flame. He stirred a teaspoonful of pulverized white sugar into the mixture, added a twist of lemon peel, and shoved the smoking concoction across the bar to the booted and bewhiskered giant. "Sir!" said Professor Thomas, bowing, "the Blue Blazer!"

It is reported that the forty-niner threw the concoction back, stood for ten seconds transfixed, then shivered like an aspen in a storm, and finally, with an uncertain grin, coughed up the following words of praise: "You done it! Yes, sirree, you gone and done it, goddam, right down to my gizzard! Yes, sirree, right down to my gizzard!" He then, the legend says, flung a heavy bag of gold dust on the counter as a token of appreciation and staggered off, a trifle unsteady, but satisfied.

During an embassy party of the 1950s, a far-gone Russian attaché insisted that Pushkin had invented the cocktail.

SELLING STRONG WATERS:
Early American taverns

Taverns in early America frequently served as a courthouse. Some of the Salem witch trials took place in a gin mill.

The Bell-in-Hand, just off Haymarket Square in Boston, claims to be the oldest continuously operating tavern in the United States and is proud of having been able to hold on to its original bar. It dates from the 18th century. There are a good number of other places that claim to be the oldest. Some venerable structures go back to the late 1600s, but have not been in business uninterruptedly.

In Boston, the Cole House, founded in 1634, was supposed to be the oldest ordinary in town that had been built as such. Houses that doubled as tippling places dispensed liquor as early as 1625. In the Cole House, Chief Miantonomoh and 20 of his warriors were plied with brandy, addling their brains sufficiently to let themselves be persuaded to sign a treaty that deprived them of their lands.

For heroic deeds on behalf of the early settlers, a Captain Willard was given a monopoly to "sell wine and strong waters" in Concord, Massachusetts, *anno Domini* 1636. Little did the good captain know that one of his direct descendants, Frances Willard, would become a leader of the Prohibition movement.

At Williamsburg, Virginia, the inventory of Burdette's ordinary consisted of "one old fiddle, one billiard table with stick, balls, etc., 11 pair of dice, a quantity of choice old Madeira, and old Barbadoes Rum." Also at Williamsburg, the Red Lion tavern received a license on condition "not to suffer any person to tipple or drink more than necessary."

To drink only "as much as necessary" was a matter of judgment, and even Thomas Jefferson's judgment could be clouded at times. Drinking ale from pewter tankards and Madeira from handsome glass goblets at the Raleigh Tavern for the better part of a night, Jefferson wrote afterward, "I never could have thought the succeeding Sun would have seen me so wretched."

Evening entertainment at a local inn

The custom in New England was to give a license to a tavern only if it was conveniently close to a church. The predicament of Jacob Upton and Jedediah Cooper of Fitchburg, Massachusetts, was that they had a tavern, but no church. After pondering the problem for 10 years they simply put up a meeting house themselves, a crude structure they called "the Lord's Barn."

In early Knickerbocker Town, Director-General Kieft faced a difficult predicament. English sailors staying at New Amsterdam did not readily take to the ways, lingo, or beverages of the Dutch burghers and frequently provoked bloody fights. Kieft therefore had the Stadt Herberg ("City Tavern") built—a sturdy stone structure—and, for a while, one half was reserved for the Dutch, who sat stolidly quaffing Schiedam schnapps and geneva, while blowing smoke rings from their long, white clay pipes, and in the other half, the British tars downed tumblers of Kill-Devil and brandy, threw dice, and danced the jig on tabletops.

Toward the end of Peter Stuyvesant's rule, the city had become very cosmopolitan. It was said that one could hear 16 different languages spoken in New Amsterdam's taverns. Then, as now, the city was easygoing on the foibles of tourists. A Dutch sailor, who was about to be punished for being smashed, pointed out that "at Mannadoes [Manhattan] they were not punished for drunkenness but used after they had been drunk to say, 'God forgive us,' or 'Be merciful to us,' and that was enough."

One of the earliest New York alehouses was the White Horse Tavern, run by a Frenchman, and since his time there have always been White Horse saloons in New York.

The early settlers were always in a hurry to have a tippling place, so much in a hurry that at Philadelphia they brought the ready-hewn timbers for a tavern with them on their ship. The timbers were used to build a 12-by-22-foot structure, filled in with bricks, known as the Anchor tavern. It was later renamed the Boatman and Call, and still later the Blue Anchor, under which name it became famous.

By the time William Penn arrived in Philadelphia, there were already 3 rum mills in operation, one of them the Penny Pot House and Landing, which, true to its name, sold ale and beer at 1 penny a pot. It was a two-story brick building and was later called the Jolly Tar Inn. In 1683 William Penn wrote that Philadelphia had 7 ordinaries where a good meal could be had for 6 pence.

The City Tavern, a pouring spot frequented by George Washington, who liked its Hot Buttered Rum, advertised in 1774 that it had "a long room, divided into boxes, fitted with tables, and elegantly lighted."

When Benjamin Franklin arrived in Philly in 1723, the first thing he did was to lift one at the Crooked Billet. Many years later Franklin's own house became a tavern, and he had the further honor of having at least 2 dozen inns and dramshops named after himself, which was only fitting for one who poetically had extolled the virtues of winebibbing.

Some tavern keepers kept smoked and heavily salted codfish in kegs next to their barrels of booze, encouraging customers to help themselves freely and without charge. The codfish, of course, engendered a mighty thirst, which could only be quenched with generous helpings of ale or rum.

Not a few towns were named after taverns. In Pennsylvania's Amish country, not far from each other, are the townships of Bird-in-Hand, Blue Ball, and Intercourse. The first was named after a tavern displaying a sign with the legend "A Bird in the Hand Is worth two in the Bush." The second was named after a taproom displaying two large blue balls as its sign. The third was first called Cross Keyes, after an ordinary of that name. In 1813 it was renamed Intercourse, after the Jolly Intercourse Inn. (Ralph Ginzburg, publisher of the elegant, soft-core but hardcover magazine *Eros*, tried to have *Eros* mailed from Intercourse for the sake of the postmark. It was one of the charges brought against him in an obscenity case that he lost.)

Early American taverns, following English tradition, had colorful names and signs: the Star Chamber, Bull's Head, the Crown and Eagle, Pig and Whistle, Unicorn, and Catamount. The Bag o' Nails was a favorite, originally the Bacchanalians. Some of the strange tavern names were due to the fact that the more sophisticated ones were changed into more colloquial words. God Encompasseth Us became Goat and Compass. The Pique et Carreau ("Spades and Diamonds") eventually became the Pig and Carrot.

Some taverns were simply named after their owners: Cole House, Fraunces Tavern, or Buckman's, which later became Longfellow's famous Wayside Inn. Its taproom was called the "coop," as it was a cagelike structure resembling a henhouse.

The Hen and Chickens tavern at Lancaster had a sign proclaiming, "May the Wings of Liberty Cover the Chickens of Freedom, and Pluck the Crown from the Enemy's Head."

The old-time tavern keeper was called "mine host," "Ganymede," "publican," "tapster," "tapper of strong drink," "hostler," or, most often, "landlord."

The early landlords were usually men of consequence and means, given their license for being "sober in mind and conversation." The first tavern in Cambridge, Massachusetts, was kept by a deacon of the church and high dignitary at Harvard College. The first licensed wine seller was Nicholas Danforth, a selectman and member of the high court. Sam Fraunces, a friend of George Washington and owner of the still-existing tavern in New York that bears his name, paid philosophers to lecture in his ordinary and was honored by Congress with a gift of 200 pounds in recognition of his services to the cause of liberty.

Just as customers pumped the host for news, so the host, in an eternal quest for new material, pumped the customers. Benjamin Franklin had a way to handle this. Explained one of his friends: "I have heard Dr. Franklin relate with great pleasantry that in travelling when he was young, the first step he took for his tranquility and to obtain immediate attention at the inns, was to anticipate inquiry by saying, 'My name is Benjamin Franklin. I was born in Boston. I am a printer by profession, am travelling to Philadelphia, shall have to return at such a time, and have no news. Now, what can you give me for dinner?'"

A strange backwoods publican was "Devil" Dave Miller of Lancaster, Pennsylvania. Immensely fat and big, he rode a ridiculously small horse, which he would trot right into his taproom to get "a snort for man and beast." The horse is said to have accepted nothing but Monongahela rye whiskey. When Devil Dave wanted to dismount, he rode into the doorway, hung by his hands from the transom, and let the horse walk out from under him to its stable.

One eccentric innkeeper, James Akin, at Newburyport, Massachusetts, was also an artist. In 1812 he had a big fight with one Edmund Blunt, who hurled a skillet at Akin. The landlord revenged himself by manufacturing chamberpots bearing Blunt's likeness and did a land-office business in the general neighborhood.

RAW ONIONS AND NO LADIES: Drinking in old New York, Chicago, and New Orleans

In 1835 New York City had 750 saloons serving 200,000 inhabitants.

Many early New York saloons coyly dubbed themselves "Oyster Cellars." These places were particularly thick on Broadway, Canal Street, and along the waterfront. For 12 cents a man was allowed to eat as many oysters as he could, washing them down with a free mug of beer or ale. Some of these places arranged oyster-shucking contests on which large sums were bet.

Harry Hill's Saloon on Houston Street was a favorite watering hole for politicos, racing fans, gambling men, and celebrities. It had separate entrances for men and women. Harry had installed a boxing ring on the second floor, and it was there that the great John L. Sullivan fought his first fight, knocking out Steve Taylor in 2 rounds. The house fighter was a Maori called Slade, and Bill Muldoon, later Sullivan's manager, wrestled all comers.

Harry Hill was the first to install electric light in his saloon, which he then renamed Harry Hill's Electric Light Hall. Hill's was a must for out-of-towners: Oscar Wilde was a regular customer.

In the 1880s and 1890s there were 6 saloons for every street block in the Bowery, 1 for every 205 inhabitants. By comparison there was a church or synagogue for every 1,000 citizens.

On New York's Cherry Street was the Turtle Tavern, a tippling house kept by a giant black woman called the Turtle or Big Sue. She weighed 375 pounds and was "not a person to fool with." She, and her dive, got their nicknames because contemporaries insisted that she looked like an enormous black turtle standing on its hind legs.

Mose Humphreys was a famous bartender on New York's Bowery during the 1840s and 1850s. He was also a printer and fireman. Forty barrels of beer were set aside yearly for his own personal use. It was said that he always kept 12 gallon jugs on his back bar, punctually emptying 1 every hour.

McGuirk's gin mill, called Suicide Hall, was so named because its owner boasted that more female alcoholics committed suicide in his establishment than in any other.

The Hoffman House bar was a wonder of marble columns and potted palms. The Hoffman House gave birth to the Manhattan cocktail.

At Mould's bar a cosmopolitan crowd and New York's literati enjoyed a rich bean soup gratis together with the house's famous Razzle-Dazzle cocktail made of brandy, ginger ale, and absinthe.

"Papa" Smith's Silver Dollar saloon had 1,000 silver dollars imbedded in its floor, 500 more hanging from the chandeliers, and 500 more used ornamentally behind the bar.

Lüchow's, still in business on 14th Street, is probably the only place in New York with a bar that boasts a stuffed buffalo head. Lüchow's was the spot where Diamond Jim Brady demolished gargantuan meals, sometimes in the company of Lillian Russell. One U.S. senator, when dining with his wife, would always order a cup of oyster-juice soup. The knowing Lüchow's waiters would quickly appear with a cupful of bonded whiskey. The wife never caught on.

The first tavern and drinking place in Chicago was a crude two-story log cabin owned by Mark Beaubien. It opened for business in 1831 and was called Sauganash in honor of a Potawatomi Indian chief. Also known as Jolly Mark's Inn after its red-faced, fat owner, who always wore a blue, brass-buttoned swallowtail coat, it had a sort of porch from which guests could take occasional shots at waterfowl, passing deer, and even bears, whose meat, not infrequently, wound up on the dinner table.

McSorley's Old Ale House is the oldest of the typical pre-Civil War saloons still operating in New York City. It was founded in 1854 by an Irish immigrant. McSorley's was one of the last "for men only" drinking establishments. For over a century it displayed signs reading "Good ale, raw onions and no ladies," and "No Back Room in Here for Ladies." In the wake of the feminist movement, McSorley's was sued for sexism and had to open its doors to women on August 10, 1970.

McSorley's is the only true alehouse left in the world—the only liquid refreshment sold is ale. When asked why he never sold anything else (or stronger), such as whiskey, John McSorley, the founder, explained, "Ale and porter is potent enough for any man."

Mickey Finn was the name of a murderous and thieving saloon owner who kept the Lone Star Saloon and Palm Garden on Chicago's Whiskey Row and gave his name to the famous knockout concoction that was first used in his joint to knock out unfortunate customers in order to rob them. A black voodoo shaman, who sold love potions and aphrodisiacs along the Row, as well as opium to addicts, once approached Mickey with a "bottle of white stuff"—later identified as chloral hydrate—saying it was better than any knockout drops known. It was. Finn put up a sign on his back bar reading "Try a Mickey Finn Special," and the women working his saloon sold the stuff to customers on a percentage basis. The Special was a mixture of raw alcohol, snuff, and Doctor Hall's white stuff. If the Special did not fell its man, Mickey would roar, "Give him a Number Two, free!" Number Two was strong beer, tobacco, and Doc Hall's miracle potion.

When the gangster and bootlegger Al Capone was buried in a silver-plated coffin covered with $20,000 worth of flowers, all saloons in Chicago closed for 2 hours as a sign of mourning.

Chicago saloons were usually built at a corner, with entrances on both streets for better getaways.

New Orleans played a big role in the history of American drinking and drinking places. Locals claim that the Old Absinthe House was the first saloon on the continent. The city is the home of the Mardi Gras and is the birthplace of jazz, the Sazerac and the Ramos Gin Fizz cocktails, the concert saloon, the barrelhouse, as well as the free lunch.

The barrelhouse (New York also claims to have sired it) was strictly a guzzle shop, and a low one at that. It was usually a long, narrow, dark, and dank cavern with a battery of barrels lined up against one wall. For 5 cents a customer could draw his favorite tipple from one of the barrels into a good-sized mug or shot glass taken from a bin. If he did not refill promptly, he was shown the door. Usually what was stenciled on the barrels had no relationship to what they actually contained. The barrelhouse boss not only adulterated his wet goods, he also kept on hand a passel of thieves who rolled the tottering lushes after they left the groggery.

The famous institution known as the "free lunch" was conceived in 1838 by Monsieur Enrique Martinez, manager of the City Exchange saloon of New Orleans. Martinez kept a table laden with smoked oysters, barbecued pork, and his own invention, Louisiana Gumbo, kept warm by means of large silver bowls filled with hot water. Customers who paid for one drink were entitled to help themselves to these delicacies—gratis.

The smallest coin in old New Orleans was the picayune, worth 5 cents. It paid for a glass of red wine, a shot of bourbon, or a mint julep. Later, as the free lunch at the City Exchange pulled in an enormous number of new customers, other drinking places in New Orleans also began to treat customers who had spent 1 picayune to free "soups, fish, roast joints, fowls, and salad, bread and cheese."

From New Orleans the custom of treating patrons to free lunches spread, first to San Francisco and then to the rest of the country.

The Old Absinthe House in New Orleans, a high-class and genteel tippling resort for over a century, numbered among its guests Andrew Jackson and the pirate Jean Laffite. William Howard Taft was also a client. The proprietor had a hard time finding a chair that would accommodate Taft's ample posterior. Aaron Burr and a Romanoff grand duke sampled the place's liquid attractions, and Victor Herbert wrote a song about the Absinthe House's most famous offering—Absinthe Frappé. Louis Philippe, sometime king of France, is said to have tried it here, too.

The New Orleans saloon La Bourse de Maspero, also known as Maspero's Exchange, was a favorite hangout of business men and prosperous merchants. It was here that, in 1812, Andrew Jackson planned the defense of the city. Maspero's had a 90-foot bar.

The Conclave Saloon was a great tourist attraction of 19th-century New Orleans. Its back bar was an exact reproduction of a typical Louisiana above-ground burial vault, complete with marble slabs labeled "Brandy, Whiskey, Gin, Rye, etc." The bartenders were dressed as undertakers and served drinks out of bottles kept in small, silver-handled coffins.

NO MORE THAN FIVE IN ONE BED:
The Old West saloon

After the War of the Revolution, civilization advanced across the Alleghenies at the rate of 1 tavern and drinking place every 20 miles.

The early taverns of the West—and the West was at first anything beyond the Alleghenies and the Ohio River—had very little in common with the cozy New England ordinary. Western taverns were often mere huts "more fit for savages than for Christians."

Most early taverns served as civic center, courtroom, church, political gathering place, eatery, hotel, undertaker's parlor, and entertainment center, as well as stable and watering place for horses. Of course, a tavern's first and foremost business was always drinking.

The rules of one typical tavern, posted at the door, were:
Four pence a night for bed.
Six pence with supper.
No more than five in one bed.
No boots and spurs to be worn in bed.
Organ grinders to sleep in the wash house.
No razor grinders or tinkers taken in.
These, incidentally, were the rules not for a wilderness tavern, but for a city inn.

One foreign visitor complained in 1833, "The Americans possess a most singular taste for marring the beauty of every place which can boast of anything like scenery, by introducing a bar-room into the most romantic and conspicuous spot."

The Setting Hen tavern on the Wisconsin River had a landlord who was also a coffin maker and offered burial services for a fee. The river was swift and many raftsmen were drowned trying to ford it. The coffin business was thriving. The whiskey business, too. Guests had a good look at the array of coffins lined up in the taproom, sometimes occupied by a greenish, opalescent corpse, and quickly asked for another throat-duster, and then another, and then another. After all, they still had to cross the river.

The beauty of the Mississippi was marred, and the life and wallets of travelers on the river endangered, by outfits like Wilson's Liquor Vault & House of Entertainment, the Cave in the Rock, and the Hole in the Wall. These were places, sometimes caverns, disguised as saloons but in reality robbers' nests whose managers were murderous bandits who lived from plundering wayfarers. Sometimes they went so far as to sink ships moored at the riverbank in order to get at the passengers.

The famous naturalist John James Audubon used to smuggle whiskey on Mississippi River steamboats.

Mike Fink was a famous flatboat man, scrapper, and whiskey guzzler. He was once engaged in a shooting match in which he and his rival competed in shooting full whiskey glasses from the top of each other's heads. Fink missed intentionally and shot the other man dead, paying off an old grudge, some say. Fink was the subject of many whiskey legends. He is said, for instance, to have swallowed a whole buffalo robe with its hair on to serve as a new stomach lining, his old, original one having been destroyed by drinking oceans of Monongahela rye.

Sometime around 1845 or so an unknown genius decided to change the name of the American tippling place from tavern, inn, or road-ranch to "saloon" in order to give the old thirst parlor class. The idea was most likely spawned in New Orleans, for *saloon* is probably a rendition of the French *salon.*

The saloon's symbol was the famous—or infamous—"bat-wings," the swinging doors. These became so sinister a symbol that even today they are still outlawed in some states and localities—as is the word *saloon* as a designation for a drinking place.

After repeal of Prohibition, the liquor interests wanted people to forget the "old bad saloon." For a while they brought back the hoary word *tavern.* But *tavern* did not take on. *Café* was then tried, and American cities are still full of Shamrock, Harp, Blarney Stone, and Green Isle cafés, though what these establishments sell is not coffee.

Western watering troughs came in a number of varieties. A "bit house" was a place where a shot of the red essence cost a bit—25 cents. A "short-bit house" was the usual poor cowpoke's drinking place that sold whiskey at 10 cents a shot. A "barrelhouse" dispensed liquid TNT from open barrels. A "hog ranch" was a saloon in which "soiled doves" sold their favors to woman-starved boozers. A "shebang" was a jug house hastily put together out of green lumber. A "deadfall" was a very low type of saloon. "Hell on wheels" was a rolling establishment, a bar set up inside a railroad car that followed railroad workers as they laid the tracks.

Unclad classical gods and goddesses adorned the walls of the Teller House bar at Central City, Colorado. One goddess lacked a breast, another had two left feet. The artist, an Englishman, had been paid in room, board, and whiskey, and was said to have imbibed a little too much of the latter while at work.

The Boilermaker that inspired such high-flown poetry was simply a shot glass of straight whiskey chased with the Helper—a mug of cold beer.

When court was in session in Wisconsin's Hawk's Tavern and no lawyer could be found anywhere, the judge ordered the barkeep to act as attorney for the accused.

The typical western saloon was a log cabin with a large "false front" that made it look twice as big as it really was. In front of most saloons was a wooden boardwalk. Without it, customers would have sunk knee-deep in the mud.

The western saloons were known by many names: whoop-up, cantina, jughouse, watering hole, bug house, pulqueria, pouring spot, hop joint, doggery, sala, and snake ranch, to list but a few.

Besides the Saturday Night Art (oils and chromolithographs of undraped female forms), there was, after 1880, Anheuser-Busch's *Custer's Last Stand*, the most popular example of saloon art ever.

The famed Montana cowboy artist Charlie Russell began his career by selling his pictures to saloon keepers for food and drink—mostly red likker.

Many western snake ranches had towels hanging at regular intervals from the edge of the bar, thoughtfully placed there so that gents could, from time to time, wipe the beer foam, whiskey drippings, and tobacco juice from their luxuriant beards. Floors

were sanded or covered with sawdust, also to catch the assorted drippings and spittings.

The sign over a Georgetown, Colorado, saloon for a long time bore the legend "We serve the very WORST liquor," a joke played on the illiterate owner by an underpaid sign painter. It brought in so many customers that the saloon keeper left it hanging even after he found out what it meant.

Possibly the most famous of all saloon nudes—and the most expensive—were those sporting with lecherous fauns at the Hoffman House bar in New York. Painted by the French artist Adolphe William Bouguereau, they had cost the staggering sum of $10,000.

The first bottomless dancers in America appeared in 1869 in a saloon on San Francisco's Pacific Street.

At Johnny Harmon's Chicago bar the back bar had a poster: "Gentlemen will please keep their hands off the waiter girls, as it interferes with the discharge of their duties." As a result, poor Harmon went broke. His customers forsook him for Ike Bloom's place, advertised as the "dance saloon where everything goes."

When world champion John L. Sullivan and his sweetheart of the evening were refused entrance to a Chicago drinking place because "no ladies are allowed in this establishment," the great John L. roared, "When a lady is with me, she ain't no lady!"

During gold-rush days many bars had jewelers' scales on the counter to weigh the gold dust with which some miners paid for their drinks. The usual price for a double shot of whiskey was a "pinch"—as much dust as the bardog could hold between thumb and forefinger without making a hog of himself.

A saloon keeper in early California entertained his patrons with the sight of the severed head of the robber and murderer Joaquin, preserved in alcohol in a pickle jar. It cost $1 to see it. A Deadwood, South Dakota, saloon of the 1870s preserved and exhibited the head of a Sioux Indian for 2 bits a look-see.

The longest bar on record was at Erickson's, a lumbermen's establishment in Portland, Oregon. The bar measured 684 feet. Erickson's also had the first far-West all-female orchestra.

Tortoni's in Denver, Colorado, had two marble bars opposite each other. Also in Denver was the Albany Saloon, with an unbroken counter 110 feet long.

The smallest bar in Denver, Colorado, was in Walker's Saloon. The bar was long enough to accommodate 6 customers squeezed together.

Horseback imbibing was popular with many cowboys. An eastern drummer in a western bar complained when a cowboy rode his horse into the joint and the animal dumped manure on his shiny patent-leather shoes. "Stranger," said the barkeeper, "what are you doin' afoot in here, anyhow?"

Spencer Penrose was a gentleman who fully enjoyed drinking with his horse. He not only rode his horse into booze parlors, but also demanded a drink for the beast. What's more, the horse always downed its large glass of the red essence. When the bardog in the Antler's Hotel, Colorado, refused entrance to the mounted Penrose, Penrose exclaimed, "I'll damn well build by own place where they'll serve me and my horse, too." He then proceeded to erect the famous Broadmoore Hotel.

In almost every saloon there was a mirror behind the bar. It was there for a good purpose. It enabled the barkeep to keep an eye on the customers even when his back was turned to reach for a bottle or mix up a fancy drink. With the type of patrons he had to serve, watchfulness was often a matter of life or death.

San Francisco had every imaginable kind of drinking place, from tents and dugouts to ornate booze palaces. A group of sailors ran their ship aground and made a stampede for the gold fields. The abandoned vessel was promptly converted into a whiskey mill. It was called the Apollo Saloon.

It was estimated during the days of the gold rush that 1 out of every 10 Californians was a saloonist or made his or her living from employment in a grogshop.

Sidney Town was a part of San Francisco peopled by Australian convicts and deportees and was the locale of many of the lowest joints. Among these was the Boar's Head, which featured porn shows involving a naked Chilean woman and a grunting boar, and the Goat and Compass, whose prize exhibit was one steady customer, Dirty Tom McAlear, who boasted of not having washed or taken a bath for 15 years, and who was claimed to have been on a permanent 7-years' drunk without once having sobered up. The Fierce Grizzly was a saloon named after its pet, a huge live bear tethered at the entrance. The joint was famous for its milk punches, laced with strong rotgut and knockout drops.

Spencer Penrose sharing a compotation with his horse

Breen's on Market Street claims to have the longest bar in San Francisco (but not in the country)—70 feet of polished carved wood.

The perils of group inebriation

Among the attractions of some of San Francisco's saloons were the Waddling Duck, an overweight damsel who could sing in two keys at once; Lady Jane Grey, left-handed daughter of a British peer and, as she always maintained, a claimant to the British throne; the Roaring Gimlet, a skinny runt of a woman with the voice of a bullfrog; and the Little Lost Chicken, who could sing only one song: "The boat lies high, and the boat lies low/She is a-sailing on the wide O-hi-oooohhhh." What the Little Lost Chicken lacked in repertoire, she made up for by being one of the most accomplished pickpockets in town.

Hoffman's Cafe, which under the management of Pop Sullivan is said to have survived the Great Earthquake to rise phoenixlike in a new form, claims to be the oldest continuously operating bar in San Francisco. Its venerable old bar was shipped around the Horn before the arrival of the transcontinental railroad. Hoffman's has always maintained that it had the strongest drinks in town.

Westerners "bellied up to the bar" and "nominated their poison." The poison in 9 cases out of 10 was straight whiskey.

Not a few western bartenders were women. According to one chronicler, "Maggie—the Holy Terror—owned a bar in Frisco. She was one of those formidable dames who subdued obstreperous patrons with her teeth. A man could holler for mercy and then leave the premises quietly and quickly, but one customer, a mucho hombre, would not declare himself beaten, even with Maggie's choppers fastened upon one of his ears.

"'Had enough?' Maggie growled from between clenched teeth.

"'Go ahead, bite it off,' said the man, 'I can hear without it.'"

Famous gunfighters and lawmen, such as Wyatt Earp, Bat Masterson, Ben Thompson, King Fish, Doc Holliday, Wild Bill Hickok, and Bill Tilghman were all, at some time or another, saloon owners or bartenders.

The youngest barkeep in the West was 13-year-old Fred Lambert at Cimarron, Colorado. His youth was said to have a quieting influence on rough characters.

The oldest bardog on record was one Pierre, half French and half Sioux, who was still pouring them for the boys in a Nebraska saloon at the advanced age of 101.

The saloons in the West often served as stage for a play or opera. Sarah Bernhardt, Helena Modjeska, Edwin Booth, Lotta Crabtree, Maurice Barrymore, Lola Montez (ex-mistress of the king of Bavaria), and Ada Menken all performed in western saloons.

Oscar Wilde lectured Leadville miners on the beauties of interior decoration—in kneepants. His lecture was interrupted by the hanging of two road agents in front of the saloon. The miners did not get much out of the lecture, but they admired Wilde mightily, because he drank them all under the table during a drinking bout.

Probably the most notorious saloon owner and judge was Roy Bean, who held court in his Jersey Lilly saloon at Langtry, Texas. Bean was known as "the Law West of the Pecos," and he usually opened procedures with these words: "Gents, this honorable court is now in session, and if any of you gander-eyed galoots wants a snort afore we start, let him step up to the bar and name his brand."

Ice was not available in the back country until fairly late. Roy Bean, judge and booze boss, used to stir a piece of glass in his drinks—just for show.

Oscar Wilde and his students

Judge Roy Bean's saloon was situated next to the railroad station. Trains stopped there twice daily for 10 minutes, and the parched passengers usually availed themselves of the occasion to get a drink at the judge's place. Bean never, absolutely never, gave one of these customers change. He always delayed matters until the whistle blew and the train was about to pull out, forcing the travelers to hotfoot it to the station if they did not want to miss the train and be stranded in the middle of nowhere. Those who raised objections usually lost.

SENATORIAL THIRST:
Liquor and Washington, D.C.

The first saloon in the newly established District of Columbia was the Indian Queen, much beloved by the lawgivers. Its sign was a rather gaudy picture of Pocahontas. Senator Randolph of Virginia made his headquarters in the Indian Queen because, so he said, he was one of Pocahontas's descendants. Flagons of brandy, rum, and whiskey were put on the members' dinner tables; they were to help themselves gratis to as much of the stuff as they liked or could hold. They could hold a lot, and soon men began to speak of "senatorial thirst."

Behind the bar of the Indian Queen was a row of bells. Over each one was a number indicating a room occupied by a congressman. When the congressman pulled the string, the bell started to ring. The numbers of rings denoted the kind of liquid refreshment desired, which was immediately rushed to the guest's room.

George Washington spent more on liquor than any other man in the country. He had, naturally, a lot of entertaining to do, but then he did a lot of his own brewing and distilling on his Mount Vernon plantation. At Valley Forge he bemoaned the fact that he had only vile, raw whiskey to serve to his guests.

Thomas Jefferson was partial to good French wines, punch, Madeira, and American-brewed ales and beers.

Thomas Jefferson was a connoisseur of good wine. He spent roughly $11,000 on wine while at the White House, and was a genial host. In his diary and letters, he kept track of the various wines he had encountered during his travels in Europe, commenting on the quality of each.

Benjamin Franklin had a curious little punch keg that he rolled around the table, from one of his guests to the next, bidding them to help themselves freely.

John Adams loved cider and had a tankard of applejack every day before breakfast, while John Quincy Adams followed Jefferson's lead, laying in a good cellar of capital French and Rhine wines.

James Madison and James Monroe were both fond of wine.

Andrew Jackson liked Tennessee whiskey. His inauguration in 1829 turned into an alcoholic orgy when the public invaded the East Room of the White House, where huge barrels of punch had been set out for the delectation of the invited guests.

Abraham Lincoln was abstemious, but he had once obtained a license to sell hard stuff in his Illinois grocery store.

John Wilkes Booth is said to have drunk heavily in a saloon before going to Ford's Theatre to assassinate the president.

Before taking the oath of office in 1865, Andrew Johnson drank tumblers of brandy. He was so unsteady on his feet during his swearing in that two senators had to support him. Afterward he made a speech so rambling and incoherent that it was termed "scandalous."

Mrs. Rutherford B. Hayes was known as "Lemonade Lucy" because she served no alcoholic beverages in the White House. It was said that at her parties "water flowed like champagne." There were, however, tables with bowls of nonalcoholic punches and fruit juices, which senators referred to as "life-saving stations." Unknown to the hostess, the lawmakers had seen to it that these stations were supplied with bottles of Old St. Croix rum.

Of McKinley it was said that "by his conspicuous example as a wine-drinker at public banquets he has done more to encourage the liquor business, to demoralize the habits of young men and to bring Christian practices into disrepute than any other President this country ever had."

Teddy Roosevelt, on some occasions, is said to have played practical jokes on teetotaling guests by slipping ardent spirits into their ginger ale. Under his administration "loose and intemperate customs ruled in the Nation's Capital."

President Taft was fond of lobster à la Newburg and Moët et Chandon or Veuve Cliquot.

Al Smith's defeat at the polls was due to his being smeared as being the champion of "Rum, Romanism, and Rebellion."

DASH THE BOWL TO THE GROUND: Temperance, Prohibition, and Repeal

Movements to curb inebriation are almost as old as the discovery of fermented juice. The Spartans forced their slaves to get drunk and then let their sons watch the helot's antics to set an example of what excessive intoxication would do to a person.

Dr. Benjamin Rush, physician and friend of George Washington, may be said to have been the father of the temperance movement in America (though pious Puritan preachers began inveighing against the sin of drunkenness as soon as they set foot on this continent). The republic had hardly been born when Rush began sermonizing against the despiritualizing effects of rum.

Early temperance advocates did not want to legislate a citizen's drinking habits. They proposed instead to reform a hard-guzzling and permanently more-or-less-stewed society by moral persuasion.

Members of abstinence societies sang "Dash the Bowl to the Ground" and signed pledges to "refrain forever from ingesting spirituous and malt liquors, wine, or cider." On some pledges a letter was put after each signature indicating how far a pledger wanted to go. *M* stood for moderation; *A* stood for abstinence from ardent spirits only; *T* stood for total abstinence, hence the expression "*t*eetotal."

Moral 'suasion did not preclude frightening the public into abstinence. Alcohol was blamed as the cause of every bodily ill, from piles to cancer. "Some are killed instantly; some die a lingering death; some commit suicide in fits of intoxication; and some are actually burned up." Indeed, drunkards were supposed to be highly combustible and to actually go up the flue in a blaze of "spontaneous combustion." Parsons and physicians loved to tell the sad tale of the gin tippler "whose breath caught fire by coming in contact with a lighted candle, and he was consumed!"

As late as the 1920s schoolmarms would do the Lord's work by showing their little students two rosy, healthy, untainted calf's brains and then pouring wood alcohol over one to let the children watch it turn into a dark, ghastly purple. "That will happen to your

Spontaneous combustion, the result of intemperance

brains," the teacher would tell the class, "if you ever touch that vile stuff called liquor!"

Persuasion was moral as well as clinical. According to one current statement: "If I be willing accessory to my brother's death, by a pistol or cord, the law holds me guilty; but guiltless if I mix his death drink in a cup. The halter is my reward if I bring him his death in a bowl of hemlock; if in a glass of spirits, I am rewarded with his purse."

There were also some catchy mottoes: "Temperate drinking is the downhill road to intemperance."

Moral persuasion was eventually abandoned for the cry "The saloon must go!" and, later, "We stand for abolition, for total prohibition!" This change in attitude was due to a number of factors, not the least of which was the fact that nondrinkers had been organizing for 50 years and the drinkers had no organization whatsoever. They had been too busy drinking.

Carry Nation was the temperance movement's wrath of God, and her weapon was the mighty hatchet. She preached the necessity of combating the rum shop not with prayers and hymns alone, but with "hatchetation."

Already past 50 when she got the call, Carry Nation looked like J. Edgar Hoover wearing a granny bonnet. She was tall and broad-shouldered, muscular and well-padded fore and aft. It took 4 policemen to subdue her when she was on a rampage.

Speaking of herself in the third person, Carry Nation said, "God gave Samson a jawbone, He gave David a sling, and He has given Carry Nation a hatchet!"

Carry Nation would snatch the cigars from the lips of passersby, snarling, "Put away this vile, stinking thing, you rummy! Glory to God!"

Carry Nation told how she heard the voice of the Lord distinctly, commanding her to "Smash, smash, in the name of Jesus, and I'll stand by you."

Carry Nation made money from selling little souvenir hatchets. As she explained, "The way I happened to think of a hatchet as a souvenir, some one brought me one and told me I ought to carry them. I then selected a pattern and got a party in Rhode Island to make them. These have been a great financial help to me. I sell them wherever I go."

One bardog stripped Carry Nation down to her underwear and pushed her out into the street in nothing but her "unmentionables." Tipplers put white mice under her skirts and pelted her with rotten eggs. The wife of one saloon keeper struck Carry a tremendous blow, knocked her down, and kicked her several times in her ample posterior. But the "bulldog at the feet of Jesus" just tied a raw beefsteak on her shiner and went on smashing. Carry thrived on persecution and gloried in martyrdom. She taunted policemen, "Arrest me, arrest me, you rum-soaked servants of Satan!" They usually obliged her.

The Budweiser people offered Carry Nation $500 if she would smash their bottles exclusively. Brewers hired brass bands to play "Welcome Carry" whenever she came to town. The "Wets" had their fun with Carry, but she had radicalized antisaloon women across the country.

There were Carry Nation Saloons in St. Louis, Leavenworth, and Chicago. One groggery named after her, in Houston, she smashed personally.

One enterprising distiller came out with Carry Nation Whiskey. It was sold in a bottle that looked very much like its namesake, emphasizing her enormous bosom and buttocks.

Temperance society pamphlets instructed young ladies how to repel advances from young swains who had imbibed: "You may not see me, John, while the breath of alcohol is on your lips. But I shall pray for you, pray to God to deliver you from this evil habit. And, if a year from now, you can say that in that time you have totally abstained, then, John, with the permission of Papa and Mama, you may call on me again."

Addressing a temperance meeting, Abraham Lincoln said, "If we take the habitual drunkards as a class, their heads and hearts will bear an advantageous comparison with those of any other. . . . The demon of intemperance seems ever to have delighted in sucking the blood of genius and generosity."

The greatest of all persuaders was a book written by T. S. Arthur in 1854 called *Ten Nights in a Barroom and What I Saw There.* The dramatic version, written by William W. Pratt in 1858, enjoyed great fame. The play depicted a whole village, Cedarville, which over a 10-year period is brought to ruin by Simon Slade's Sickle and Sheaf saloon. Mothers die of broken hearts, children expire from cruel beatings (one is killed when she is struck by a thrown glass), tipplers perish from suicide or the consequences of delirium tremens, lunatic asylums overflow and have to turn away patients, judges are debarred, and young, rich inheritors wind up in the poorhouse while young daughters escape ravishment and a fate worse than death only by divine intervention. It was a very popular play, indeed.

He rose and staggered to the bar
As oft he'd done before,
And to the landlord smiling said,
"Just fill me one glass more."

The cup was filled at his command,
He drank of the poisoned bowl,
He drank while his wife and children starved,
And ruined his own soul.

Performances always ended with the warning: "Just one drink, one small drink, is all the devil needs!"

Owen P. White wrote about *Ten Nights in a Barroom*: "This crowning effort of genius had a great run. In it, you remember, the village belle, her skirts shockingly short to make her look as if she were only ten or a quarter past, feverishly grabs the Baptist deacon by the hand, drags him dramatically across the stage, and hysterically exclaims:

Father, dear Father, come home with me now,
The clock in the steeple strikes one.

Abie's Irish Rose, with its measly record of only four years on Broadway, is not to be mentioned in the same breath with this pre-Prohibition masterpiece."

Bar scene with flying glassware

The antisaloonists did a great deal of singing. The drinkers parodied their intoning "Nearer My God to Thee " by singing "Nero, my dog, has fleas."

Drinking men sang, too. Among their favorites were "You'll Never Miss the Liquor till the Keg Runs Dry," "Everybody Works but Father," "Roll Out the Barrel," "The Old Man's Drunk Again," and "Where's My Little Pitcher of Beer?"

The following sentence appears in *Moby Dick:* "There is some sneaking Temperance Society movement about this business!"

Prohibitionism went hand in hand with the fight for women's right to vote. "When women walk to the polls, goodbye, Mr. Booze!"

Even the Father of His Country, George Washington, was found to have pronounced anathema upon intemperance: "The sure means to avoid evil is—first to refrain from drink, which is the source of all evil and the ruin of half the workmen in the country." On the other hand, Washington paid his gardener "Four dollars at Christmas with which he may be drunk for four days and nights; two dollars at Easter to effect the same purposes; two dollars at Whitsuntide to be drunk for two days; a dram in the morning and a drink of grog at noon." Not all of Washington's writings were popular with the temperance movement.

One of the reasons for the success of the prohibition movement is that the saloon had considerably deteriorated. Free enterprise was killing it: there was too much competition. Most groggeries were owned by breweries, and the booze boss was merely a franchise holder who had to sell a lot of the company's beer if he wanted to make a living and keep his franchise. In order to do this he had to break the law and sell after legal hours, on Sundays, and to minors, encouraging his customers to drink beyond the capacities of both their stomachs and their purses. He also sold bad liquor out of bottles with labels that had nothing to do with their contents.

Even avid customers complained about the booze served in local saloons. "I used to drink 50 glasses a day. Now I can barely down 10 glasses without becoming sick and having a headache all day."

Some distillers, as a sales gimmick, advertised a pack of cards and revolver free with every bottle sold.

Prominent among the evils of alcohol, of course, were the dreaded DTs, also known as "the trembles":

See how that rug those reptiles soil!
They're crawling o'er me in my bed!
I feel their clammy, snaky coil
On every limb—around my head!
With forked tongue I see them play;
I hear them hiss—tear them away!

Poison'd serpents and ugly toads, too,
Crawl on my bed their skins to shed,
Away with you, away—shooh-shooh!
Ah, they come to kill me dead!
Their forked tongues make mock of me,
Please, oh, please—take them off of me!

The "Maine-iacs" in Maine were the first to legislate their state dry, in 1846. As went Maine, so went the rest of the country. Long before national prohibition, the majority of states were already dry, and in many states that were not, numerous counties were.

Nationwide prohibition became a reality at 7:05 A.M., January 16, 1920.

In the last hours before Prohibition went into effect there was a mad rush to buy up anything alcoholic. Everywhere people could be seen lugging heavy suitcases and packages home. Streets were jammed with vehicles of every kind busy transporting the wet goods. The *New York Herald Tribune* reported the grim determination of the citizens "to hire trucks or baby carriages or anything else on wheels." The *Post* said that "probably never before had so much bottled liquor been in transit in this city."

The terrors of alcohol-created serpents

During Prohibition, liquor was smuggled in from foreign countries. At one time there were as many as 335 rumrunning vessels off the Atlantic Coast. The greatest of all rumrunners was Billy McCoy, and because his stuff was the genuine imported article, people began to say, "This is the real McCoy."

Almost all authors were against temperance and prohibition. Mark Twain, Moss Hart, Bret Harte, Dan De Quille, F. Scott Fitzgerald, H. L. Mencken, Lucius Beebe, John Asbury, Alexander Woollcott, Eugene O'Neill, and others saw in the specter of prohibition a threat to liberty.

Many American writers went to Paris to escape the ravages of Prohibition. Among them, at one time or other, Ernest Hemingway, Sherwood Anderson, George Antheil, Theodore Dreiser, Henry Miller, Sinclair Lewis, William Shirer, Ezra Pound, F. Scott Fitzgerald (to name but a few) did their writing in Paris.

Since wine is an ingredient of some Jewish religious ceremonies, rabbis were entitled to certain amounts of red wine. As a consequence the number of rabbis in New York increased tenfold.

The speakeasy got its name because one had to whisper the code word through a slot in a locked door to gain admittance. Knowing the right word or the right person carried prestige.

The yearly pay of a police captain during the years of Prohibition was $3,000, but from this sum one captain was able to save $133,845.86. A police inspector with a salary of $5,000 accumulated a nest egg of more than $193,000. It was well understood that the best speakeasies enjoyed police protection, and such protection was costly.

The word *bootlegger* originated in Kansas, bone-dry long before Prohibition, because when a moonshiner went to peddle his illegal booze, he carried it in pint bottles stuck in his high boots.

The manufacturers of certain brands of antifreeze and hair tonics became millionaires when people discovered that their products contained alcohol that could be used to make booze. Antifreeze was actually allowed to do legitimate duty in radiators before being used as drink, as it was thought that rust and iron improved its potability.

Scat Whiskey, Blue John, Old Stinko, Happy Sally, and Soda Pop Moon were a few of the frightful concoctions made of melted canned heat, rubbing alcohol, and other deadly substances.

Chock beer was very popular during Prohibition. It consisted of blackstrap molasses, yeast, water, and corn pone. It was allowed to sit and ferment for 3 weeks. It was then strained and bottled and was ready to be swallowed. Also known as Old Hen, it was a deplorable drink, but fearfully potent.

One particularly fatal misapprehension was that denatured alcohol, such as used in antifreeze, could be made drinkable after having been filtered through a loaf of bread.

At 7:00 P.M. Washington time, December 5, 1933, President Franklin D. Roosevelt signed the proclamation ending Prohibition. After 13 years, 10 months, and 18 days, America was wet again.

Both Russia and Iceland had prohibitions that lasted longer than America's "Noble Experiment."

In Baltimore, at the bar of the Old Rennert Hotel, friends assembled to watch H. L. Mencken hoist the first mug. To their disappointment he insisted upon, before all else, drinking a glass of water—"My first in thirteen years." He then ceremoniously quaffed his beer, saying, "Pretty good, not bad at all."

When Al Smith was asked, on the morning of December 8, 1933, to pose with a glass containing alcoholic liquid, he declined with a smile, saying, "I never drink in the daytime," as America awoke with the greatest hangover ever.

EARLY RESEARCH: Facts about the author

Richard Erdoes was born in Vienna 1 year before the end of the Austro-Hungarian empire.

After the death of his father, Richard Erdoes was brought up by his uncle, an actor of some renown. This uncle sent out letters to the best liquor firms in Europe. The letters read: "Gentlemen: I am a well-known actor with an immense circle of wealthy and influential friends. I would like to represent your product among these outstanding personalities. Please send sample bottles." Wooden chests arrived in profusion, full of small bottles of the choicest liquors. Every evening the dear uncle would open some of the bottles, asking 10-year-old Richard, "Well, my boy, what will it be today for you? Danziger Goldwasser? Nuremberg Bocksbeutel? Curaçao? Cointreau? A snifter of Asbach Uralt or maybe Grand Armagnac?" Thus Richard Erdoes began his research. The uncle never made the slightest effort to sell any of the wet goods; he and the family, little Richard included, drank it all themselves. The supply lasted almost 3 years. From time to time inquiries arrived from distilleries wanting to know how their product was moving. The uncle answered them all with a form letter: "Gentlemen: Your inferior ardent spirits do not measure up to the highest standards maintained by my wealthy and influential friends. You have been a big disappointment and embarrassment to me. Please do not communicate with me further."

Richard Erdoes studied art at the academies of Vienna and Berlin, as well as at the Academie de la Grande Chaumière in Paris.

Richard Erdoes published a series of satyrical stories about the Nazis and caricatures of very un-Germanic-looking Hitlers, immensely fat Goerings, and shrunken Goebbelses, in Viennese newspapers and magazines. The Nazis saw little humor in Erdoes's efforts and put a price on his head. When the Germans marched into Austria, Erdoes fled to Paris and eventually wound up in New York, New York.

In the United States Mr. Erdoes worked mainly as a book and magazine illustrator, working for *LIFE*, *Fortune*, *The Saturday Evening Post*, *Esso Lamp*, *The Smithsonian*, *Venture*, *Esquire*, and many other publications.

Mr. Erdoes has received many awards at exhibitions of the Art Director's Club of New York, the American Institute of Graphic Arts, and the Society of Illustrators.

Erdoes took to serious writing in 1970 and has published 12 books since then, some of which have been translated into many foreign languages. Among his works are *Lame Deer: Seeker of Visions; The Woman Who Dared; Saloons of the Old West; The Sound of Flutes; The Sun Dance People;* and *The Rain Dance People.*

Richard is married to Jean, a fellow artist he met at *LIFE*. They have 2 sons, 1 an artist and designer, the other a film editor, and 1 daughter, a teacher.

The entire Erdoes family has been heavily involved in American Indian civil rights, has lived with Indians, and has written books about and with native Americans.

Richard and his family are enthusiastic hikers, campers, skiers, and photographers. They divide their time between their New York studio and Santa Fe, New Mexico.

All the money e'er I had
I spent it in good company;
And all the harm I've ever done,
Alas! it was to none but me.
And all I've done for want of wit
To memory now I can't recall:
So fill to me the parting glass,
Goodnight, and joy be with you all.

If I had money enough to spend
And leisure time to sit awhile,
There is a fair maid in this town
That sorely has my heart beguiled.
Her rosy cheeks and ruby lips
I own she has my heart in thrall,
Then fill to me the parting glass,
Goodnight and joy be with you all.

Oh, all the comrades e'er I had
They're sorry for my going away:
And all the sweethearts I e'er had
They'd wish me one more day to stay,
But since it falls unto my lot,
That I should rise and you should not;
I gently rise and softly call—
Goodnight and joy be with you all.